CANADIAN HERITAGE COLLECTION

CANADIAN-AMERICAN RELATIONS

Charles Leskun & Tim Tobin

Series Editor
Don Kendal

D1497322

Ru'bicon

I thank my wife, Janice, and my kids Ryan, Siobhan and Bridget for all of their understanding and patience during the research and writing of this book. I would also like to thank the staff, administration and students of St. Thomas Aquinas Secondary School in Brampton for their continued inspiration and support that is provided to me on a daily basis and makes the job of teaching Canadian history so fulfilling. Thanks all! Tim

Thank you to Karen for all her time, help, respectful commentary, love and encouragement. Charles

Rubicon © 2004 Rubicon Education Inc.

Editorial Coordinator: Martine Quibell
Project Editors: Miriam Bardswich, Kim Koh
Design: Jennifer Drew
Assistant Designer: Jeanette Debusschere

National Library of Canada Cataloguing in Publication

Leskun, Charles
    Canadian-American relations / Charles Leskun, Tim Tobin.

(Canadian heritage collection)
Includes bibliographical references and index.
ISBN 0-921156-79-0

    1. Canada—Relations—United States—Textbooks. 2. United States—Relations—Canada—Textbooks. 3. Canada—Foreign relations—United States—Textbooks. 4. United States—Foreign relations—Canada—Textbooks. I.Tobin, Tim. II. Title. III. Series: Canadian heritage collection (Oakville, Ont.)

FC249.L467 2003   303.48'271073   C2003-900355-8
F1029.5.U6L47 2003

Printed in Canada

COVER
© Michael S. Yamashita/CORBIS/Magmaphoto.com

Table of Contents

Introduction   4

1776 – 1899   6

1900 – 1919   8

1920 – 1929   14

1930 – 1939   18

1940 – 1949   20

1950 – 1959   24

1960 – 1969   28

1970 – 1979   32

1980 – 1989   36

1990 – 1999   40

Into the 21st Century   44

Index   48

INTRODUCTION

"Geography has

made us neighbours,

history has made us

friends, economics

has made us partners

and necessity has

made us Allies.

Those who nature

has put together let

no man put asunder."

— John Fitzgerald
Kennedy, address to
Canadian Parliament,
1961

THE BORDER BETWEEN Canada and the United States has been referred to as "the world's longest undefended border." This speaks volumes about the nature of the relationship between the two nations. It is a relationship that has had both tests and triumphs; yet one that remains our most important with any foreign power. Canada is very different – in values, in policies, and in actions – from the United States; yet our political, defence, economic, and cultural concerns remain inextricably tied to them.

Author Seymour Lipset referred to the American Revolution as a "formative event" in the history of both nations. It led to the birth of the United States, a nation that created a government purposely different from its British predecessor. It brought to the north a group of refugees determined to maintain its heritage as British North America. The United Empire Loyalists brought political and social baggage designed to ensure that the Canadian colonies would remain British both in name and in tradition.

The two competing continental visions clashed on numerous occasions in the 19th century. The clashes were sometimes diplomatic, often commercial, and occasionally violent. Within a generation of the birth of the United States, it had declared war on its British North American neighbour. The war had a big impact on both nations. The British attack on Baltimore and Washington provided the inspiration for a new American national anthem and a new name for the President's residence. By repelling attacks in both Upper and Lower Canada, the colonies had passed a test of nationhood – both the French and English communities had fought to remain part of British North America. Both sides were determined to live at peace with each other, and signed an agreement to remove all warships from the Great Lakes.

By the mid point of the 19th century, new issues had emerged to test the relationship. The Monroe Doctrine, American Manifest Destiny, slavery and the Underground Railroad, and the American Civil War had profound effects on both American and Canadian consciousness. In response to a growing American aggression regarding continental and hemispheric expansion, Canada continued to assert her sovereignty and distinctiveness. Following the violence and sectional discord of the Civil War, Canada created a federal Constitution designed to avoid a similar misfortune. The American struggle with strong states maintaining residual powers, for instance, would not be repeated here. The British North America Act was a constitution moulded by the desire to remain British, to learn from the American experience, and to have these lessons enshrined in political arrangements that would maintain a unified country in the face of potential discord.

The settlement of Canada's West was very different from the American experience. The Canadian West was known as the "Last, Best West," in contrast to the American "Wild West." In general, the rule of law and law enforcement preceded settlement in Canada. Except for the Riel Rebellions of 1870 and 1885, there was no war between Natives and Canadian authorities. After his defeat of General Custer at the Battle of the Little Big Horn, Sioux Chief Sitting Bull found a different reality in Canada from what he would have experienced had he remained in the United States.

During the 20th century, the relationship between the two countries changed. Canada began to view itself as a North American nation, not just a re-creation of Britain in North America. Canada's diplomatic, economic, and defence policies began to reflect a growing sense of a relationship with the United States. The Americans were no longer viewed as potential military enemies but as allies with whom we could keep the continent safe from external threat. World War II cemented this re-orientation, while the Cold War and the aftermath of the terrorist attack of 9/11 2002 will likely keep Canada in the American military orbit for the foreseeable future.

Throughout the 20th century, and especially after the 1920s when the United States became both Canada's largest trading partner and main source of foreign investment, the wealth and standard of living of Canadians has been tied to the American economy. Trade agreements signed in the latter part of the 20th century — the Free Trade Agreement and the North American Free Trade Agreement — further linked both nations. The consequences of these commitments remain controversial in this country. Canada's ability to maintain political and social sovereignty in the light of such powerful ties will continue to be one of the most profound challenges that this nation will face. The control of such key sectors as energy, water, and other natural resources, and the maintenance of our publicly-funded health care system in the face of competition from private American health care providers, pose important challenges to our sovereignty.

Similar challenges have long fuelled concern over the expression of a distinctly Canadian culture. The rise of giant American cultural industries — movies, radio, magazines, television, and the Internet — have posed threats to Canadian cultural expression throughout the 20th century. The Canadian response has been to create public institutions like the CBC, the National Film Board, and numerous museums and public galleries, and to provide both regulation of and financial support to private cultural providers through the CRTC (Canadian Radio-Television and Telecommunications Commission) and various Arts Councils. Such public support is very different from the American approach to issues of culture.

It is in every Canadian's interest to understand the nature and meaning of our bond with the Americans. Was John F. Kennedy right? Are we in fact natural allies? If we are, what is the role that we are to play in this alliance? Are we to be merely supportive and compliant with our neighbour's continental and international policies, or are we to be truly best friends, capable of honesty when needed and affection when warranted? It is our hope that you can reach an understanding of the Canadian-American relationship by examining the primary documents in this book.

Charles Leskun and Tim Tobin

Boundary, *n.* In politics, the imaginary line between two nations, separating the imaginary rights of one country from the imaginary rights of the other.

— Ambrose Bierce, *The Devil's Dictionary,* 1911

1776 - 1899

1783	1812	1814
Treaty of Paris signed	U.S. declares war on Great Britain — invades Upper Canada	Treaty of Ghent signed, ends War of 1812

AT THE BEGINNING of the American Revolution, British holdings in North America consisted of the Thirteen Colonies along the eastern seaboard of what would become the United States; Florida East and Florida West; Nova Scotia; Cape Breton Island; St. John's Island, which later became Prince Edward Island; Newfoundland; a Quebec that included the lands along the St. Lawrence River, around the Great Lakes, and between the Appalachian Mountains and the Mississippi River; and a number of Caribbean islands. Contact among these colonies was largely confined to family connections and economic interactions that tended to be directed through London rather than within the continent itself. The political concerns that were the source of great discontent in the Thirteen Colonies seemed not to be shared to any great extent by their cousins to the north. When this discontent led to a revolution that gave birth to a new nation, efforts by the Americans to involve the others in British North America failed. Nevertheless, the impact of the American Revolution on Britain's remaining North American colonies was still being felt in the decades and even centuries that followed.

In the short term, British North America received and settled people who had remained loyal to Britain and were no longer welcome in the new Republic. For over a century, these refugees, the Loyalists, shaped how Canadians viewed American society. Their fear of American goals, government, and institutions were most powerfully experienced in the Maritimes and Ontario and helped form an attitude that was negative and occasionally hostile.

In 1812, British North America found itself under attack and fighting for its very survival. American attitudes regarding their role and entitlements in the continent and the entire Western Hemisphere, were powerfully stated in the Monroe Doctrine and Manifest Destiny. It soon became obvious to both sides, however, that British presence in North America was not about to disappear with the threat of invasion. Canadian and British reaction to both policies and the rapidly expanding American Union was one of caution and suspicion.

When the American Union was in danger of being torn apart by Civil War, Canadians observed the terrible conflict and learned not to repeat the mistakes in their own efforts at nation building. The victory of the Union over the Confederacy left a huge American army on the Canadian doorstep. This was a major impetus to Canadian Confederation.

After the Civil War and Confederation, both countries turned toward expansion across the West. Here, too, Canada and the United States followed different paths that have defined how each views itself as a distinct nation, historically, culturally, and in terms of fundamental values.

MANIFEST DESTINY

▲ *American Progress*, John Gast, 1872. In John Gast's portrayal of America's westward movement, bison herds and Indians retreat as a radiant *Manifest Destiny* — stringing telegraph wire in her wake — leads homesteaders and other settlers, wagons, and railroads across the great plains.

The American people having derived their origin from many other nations, and the Declaration of National Independence being entirely based on the great principle of human equality, these facts demonstrate at once our disconnected position as regards any other nation; that we have, in reality, but little connection with the past history of any of them, and still less with all antiquity, its glories, or its crimes. On the contrary, our national birth was the beginning of a new history, the formation and progress of an untried political system, which separates us from the past and connects us with the future only; and so far as regards the entire development of the natural rights of man, in moral, political and national life, we may confidently assume that our country is destined to be the great nation of futurity.

— John L. O'Sullivan on *Manifest Destiny*, 1839

▲ "Manifest Destiny" was a phrase used by leaders and politicians in the 1840s to explain continental expansion by the U.S. — revitalizing a sense of "mission" or national destiny for Americans.

William Seward

"I can stand here and look far off into the Northwest and see the Russian, as he busily occupies himself in establishing seaports and towns and fortifications as outposts of the Empire of St. Petersburg, and I can say, 'Go in, build your outposts to the Arctic Ocean. They will yet become the outposts of my country to extend the civilization of the United States in the Northwest.' So I look upon Prince Rupert's Land and Canada, and see how an ingenious people are occupied with bridging rivers and making railroads and telegraphs, to develop, organize, create and preserve the great British provinces of the North, by the Great Lakes, the St. Lawrence and around the shores of Hudson's Bay, and I am able to say, 'It is very well you are building excellent states to be hereafter admitted to the American Union.'"

— William Seward, Minnesota Address, 1860, from *New York Herald*, 25 January 1861

1818	1825	1854	1877
16 Apr: Rush-Bagot amendment to form unarmed U.S.-Canada border ratified	22 Feb: Russia and Britain establish Alaska/Canada boundary	Reciprocity Treaty signed between British North America and the U.S.	7 May: Sioux Chief Sitting Bull flees to Canada with 3 000 followers

A PERTINENT QUESTION

MRS. BRITANNIA – *"Is it possible, my dear, that you have ever given your cousin Jonathan any encouragement?"*

MISS CANADA – *"Encouragement: Certainly not Mamma. I have told him we can Never be United."*

CHIEF SITTING BULL

"The meat of the buffalo tastes the same on both sides of the border."— Chief Sitting Bull

"My friend, and all the Queen's men whom I so respect: I have heard of your talk. I knew you would speak to me in this way. Nobody told me. I just knew it. It is right. I came to you, in the first place, because I was being hard driven by the Americans. They broke their treaties with my people and when I rose up and fought, not against them, but for our rights, as the first people on this part of the earth, they pursued me like a dog, and would have hung me to a tree. They are not just. They drive us into war, and then seek to punish…"

— Chief Sitting Bull, submission to the terms proposed by Canadian officers, after rejecting the offers of American commissioners; quoted in Helen Hunt Jackson, *A Century of Dishonor,* 1881 (Jackson was an American author and an activist for Native American rights)

(Glenbow NB-16-566)

▲ Sioux Chief Sitting Bull, who fled to Canada after defeating Custer at the Battle of Little Big Horn in 1876.

♫ **The Bold Canadian** ♫
~ A Ballad of the War of 1812 ~

Com all ye bold Canadians,
I'd have to lend an ear
Unto a short ditty
Which will your spirits to cheer,
Concerning an engagement
We had in Detroit town,
The pride of those Yankee boys
So bravely we took down...

"For thousands of miles, the border between our two countries can be located only by consulting the stars."

— Wilfrid Laurier, Prime Minister of Canada, in a speech in Boston, 1891

◀ In the War of 1812, the invading U.S. troops were defeated with the help of British regulars and First Peoples.

The Underground Railroad

CANADA
Montreal
MAINE
St. Lawrence River
VT.
N.H.
NEW YORK
Toronto Lake Ontario
MASS. Boston
R.I. New Bedford
Buffalo
CONN.
New York
PENNSYLVANIA
N.J.
Atlantic Ocean
Baltimore
DE.
Washington, D.C. MD.
VIRGINIA

▲ The route travelled by slaves fleeing the U.S., based on Harriet Tubman's actual journeys. Using modern roads, the trip would be 900 km long. A strong, lucky runaway might have made it to freedom in two months. In bad weather, the trek might have lasted a year.

SLAVERY

"I learned the trade of a blacksmith in Kentucky. I should have been perfectly miserable to have had to work all my life for another man for nothing. As soon as I had arrived to years of discretion, I felt determined that I would not be a slave all my days. My master was a kind and honorable man; purchased no slave himself; what he had came by marriage. He used to say it was wrong to hold slaves, and a good many who hold them say the same.… I purchased my freedom, and remained in Kentucky for a while; then removed to Cincinnati thence to Chatham. Every thing goes well with me in Canada; I have no reason to complain.

I think that if a slaveholder offers his servant freedom, on condition that he will earn and pay a certain sum, and the slave accepts freedom on that condition, he is bound in honor to pay the sum promised. Some poor ignorant fellows may be satisfied with their condition as slaves, but, as a general thing, they are not satisfied with being slaves...."

— Testimony of Henry Blue, from interviews collected by Boston abolitionist Benjamin Drew who visited Canada in the 1850s and interviewed many African American refugees from the slave states

PRIME MINISTER LAURIER'S unbridled faith in the future of the country spurred Canadians to look to the future with optimism and confidence. Along with this confidence, Laurier was keenly aware of the challenges that both Britain and the United States posed for the growing nation. By 1903, Canada felt the sting of the judgment on the Alaska Boundary dispute. Canadians learned that they could not rely on Britain to protect their interests, and that the Canadian government would need to pursue international relations, especially with the Americans, on its own. This was reflected in the International Boundary Waters Treaty of 1909, which was negotiated mainly by Canadian officials with little reference to the British colonial office.

The results of the "Reciprocity" election of 1911 indicated that a majority of Canadians were unwilling to forge closer economic ties with their American neighbours. Instead, Canada chose to remain British in sentiment and protectionist in economic policy. Three years later, these political and emotional ties to the Mother Country would be reinforced with the outbreak of the Great War.

The contrast in each nation's response to war was clear. From the start, Canadians were ready and even eager to go to Britain's aid and thus prove their loyalty to the British Empire. The United States, with no emotional connection to Europe, was content to isolate itself from the European maelstrom, except for the sale of munitions and supplies to both sides. Domestic pressure forced the American government to remain neutral, especially as the war bogged down on the battlefields of France and Belgium. Americans were reluctant to sacrifice lives to solve European problems, until the sinking of the passenger liner *Lusitania* showed how vulnerable they were. As a result, by late 1917, President Wilson had changed his mind about neutrality and convinced Americans to enter the war.

World War I had significant impact on both Canada and the U.S. Canada emerged from the war as a nation with international recognition gained from the Versailles Conference. The U. S. emerged as a modern industrial giant and a world leader. However, America did not remain for long on the international stage. Despite President Woodrow Wilson's role in the Versailles peace negotiations and his championing of the League of Nations, Americans soon returned to a policy of "splendid isolationism." The U.S. Congress decided against a role in the League. While Canada did take a seat in the League, both the League and Canada's participation in it proved to be ineffectual. Nevertheless, the two North American countries drew closer economically, industrially, and culturally throughout the "Roaring Twenties."

ALASKA BOUNDARY DISPUTE

▲ **Gold rush:** Working on a claim on Bonanza Creek, Yukon, 1899. The discovery of gold in the Canadian Klondike in 1896 led to a dispute between the United States and Canada over the Alaska-Canada boundary. On 20 October 1903, the matter was settled by a tribunal of three Americans, two Canadians, and one British jurist, Lord Alverstone, who resolved the dispute when he voted in favour of the Americans.

> *"Speak softly and carry a big stick."*
> — Teddy Roosevelt on foreign policy, 1901

"...I have often regretted also that we have not in our own hands the treaty-making power which would enable us to dispose of our own affairs..."

— Sir Wilfrid Laurier, House of Commons debates, 23 October 1903

(Library of Congress)

SACRIFICED ON THE ALTAR OF DIPLOMACY TO MAKE BRITAIN SOLID WITH THE UNITED STATES.

— *The World*, Toronto, 21 October 1903

◄ Alaska-Canada border with U.S. and Canadian flags and people standing on either side, circa 1903.

The Alaskan boundary award will take its place with the Ashburton Treaty as damning evidence of Great Britain's subserviency to the United States, where the latter's interests conflict with those of Canada...the damage is irremediable. Canadians, with very few exceptions, will accept without question the statement of their representatives that their interests were sacrificed, and the resulting resentment is certain to affect the attitude of Canada towards the United States, and in still greater degree towards the motherland.

— *Manitoba Free Press*, 22 October 1903

1901

12 Dec: Guglielmo Marconi receives first transatlantic wireless message at Cabot Tower Signal Hill, Newfoundland

1903

20 Oct: Joint Commission rules in favour of U.S. in boundary dispute between District of Alaska and Canada

1903

17 Dec: Americans Wilbur and Orville Wright complete first engine-powered flight in Kitty Hawk, North Carolina

(NAC C 21425)

▲ Meeting of American and Canadian delegates (Alaska Boundary Tribunal) at the Foreign Office in London, October 1903.

"WHERE WILL THE NEXT BITE BE!"

I am very much pleased over what has just been accomplished in the Alaska Boundary award. I hesitated sometime before I would consent to a commission to decide the case... Finally I made up my mind I would appoint three men of such ability and such firmness that I could be certain there would be no possible outcome disadvantageous to us as a nation; and would trust to the absolute justice of our case, as well as to a straight-out declaration to certain high British officials that I meant business, and that if this commission did not decide the case at issue, I would decline all further negotiations and would have the line run on my own hook. I think that both factors were of importance in bringing about the result. That is, I think that the British Commissioner who voted with our men was entitled to great credit, and I also think that the clear understanding the British Government has as to what would follow a disagreement was very important and probably decisive.

— President Roosevelt in a letter to his son, 20 October 1903, *The Letters of Theodore Roosevelt*, 1951

Teddy Roosevelt

"Compliant concession to United States pretensions, Canada is well accustomed to. It formed one of the explanations of her docile acceptance of the Alaska award. Indignation had been discounted.... Everybody knew what was coming. No one, however, imagined that, this time, dishonor and treachery, rather than mere compliance, would be the principal feature attending the loss of another bit of Canadian territory...."

— John S. Ewart on the Alaska Boundary Settlement, 1903

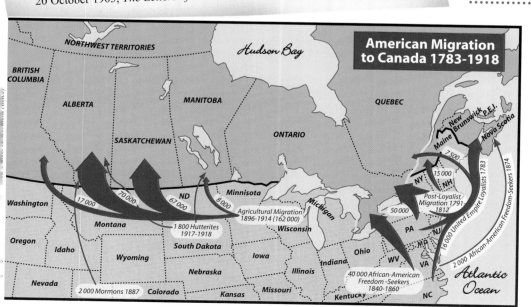

American Migration to Canada 1783-1918

A large number of immigrants from the U.S.A. are arriving, many of them originally Eastern Canadians, who have by no means realized their golden dreams of the Western States. It is to be hoped that they will leave all U.S.A. ideas behind them & realize that they have returned to a country where freedom and liberty exists for all & not for some, where law & order are respected, & where treaties with Indians are respected. A great number of these new immigrants are doing well & are heartily glad to be British citizens, but there is a remnant who would like to introduce American ideas as to what conduct "in the West" should be....

— Lady Aberdeen, diary, August 1895

NATIONAL POLICY AND BRANCH PLANTS

(The Walkerville Times)

> *Americans say of opportunity — "How much can be made of it?" Canadians say — "How little can we pay for it?"*
>
> — Agnes C. Laut, *The Canadian Commonwealth*, 1915

◄ Ford Plant in Walkerton (Windsor), Ontario, opened in 1904. By the early 1900s, the National Policy, and more specifically the tariff, encouraged many major American companies — such as The Singer Sewing Machine Company, Edison Electric, American Tobacco, Westinghouse, Gillette, International Harvester, and the Ford Motor Company — to open branch plants in Canada. By 1913, approximately 450 branches of American companies were operating in Canada.

…My only two sons…are living in a big city in the United States. My heart is aching to have them home again in some Canadian city. I am afraid they will marry American girls and settle down there… Isn't it dreadful? Divorces are so common over there. You will say, what has this got to do with the tariff? I'll tell you just what. I got a letter two weeks ago from my boys. They both work in the same factory. The letter said, 'What do you think, Mother? We may be back in Canada before long. I heard our manager say yesterday… that if our Dominion government should raise the tariff as high as the American tariff it would be necessary for our company to start a big branch factory in Canada.'…I guess there would be quite a lot of branch factories in Canada if the tariff were raised and there would be lots of work for Canadians at home. I want my boys to come home, because I think Canada is a purer and better country. They will be better men here….

— Letter to *Montreal Family Herald* and *Weekly Star,* 1903

Wilfrid Laurier

"Now our ministers at Ottawa have not the slightest desire to do anything, or to agree to anything that will have any tendency whatever to check the movement of the United States manufacturers to establish large branch plants in this country. These…establishments operate importantly to build our population and trade, and to build up a good market for the produce of our farms and it seems that the existence of our moderate tariff against the United States manufactured goods has been instrumental in bringing us these industries. Hence a strong argument exists for not meddling over much with the duties."

— Sir Wilfrid Laurier, addressing the concern of the loss of branch plants with tariff reductions under Reciprocity, quoted in *The Financial Post,* 4 June 1910

[I]t could be shown…that there is not a paper published in Canada...[that] does not deliver itself of sentiments regarding the United States which may be paraphrased thus: "We thank God we are not as thou art!"...and Canada should be thankful to God (and keep her powder dry) that crimes are punished, that innocence is protected...but it is a dangerous attitude for any people to assume toward another nation... A big ship always has barnacles; the United States is a big ship, and she keeps her engine going and her speed up and in the main her prow headed to a big destiny. It ill becomes a little ship to bark out — but let it be left unsaid!

You never mention a Jim Hill, a Doctor Osler, a Schurman, a Graham Bell — or a host of similar famous expatriates — in a Canadian gathering but some one utters with a pride of gratulation that fairly beams from the face: "They are Canadians." Canada is proud these famous men are Canadians. It has always struck me as curious that she wasn't ashamed — ashamed that she lost their services from her own nation-building. To my personal knowledge three of these men had to borrow the money to leave Canada. Their services were worth untold wealth to other lands. Their services did not give them a living in Canada….

— Agnes C. Laut, *The Canadian Commonwealth,* 1915

▶ In 1905 the International Waterways Commission was created to advise the governments of both countries about levels and flows in the Great Lakes, especially in relation to the generation of electricity by hydropower. The Boundary Waters Treaty was signed in 1909 and provided for the creation of the International Joint Commission (IJC), which has the authority to resolve disputes over the use of water resources that cross the international boundary, carry out studies requested by the governments, and advise the governments about problems.

INTERNATIONAL BOUNDARY WATERS TREATY ACT

An Act respecting the International Joint Commission established under the treaty of January 11, 1909 relating to boundary waters

Article I

The High Contracting Parties agree that the navigation of all navigable boundary waters shall forever continue free and open for the purposes of commerce to the inhabitants and to the ships, vessels, and boats of both countries equally, subject, however, to any laws and regulations of either country, within its own territory, not inconsistent with such privilege of free navigation and applying equally and without discrimination to the inhabitants, ships, vessels, and boats of both countries.

1908	1909	1910	1911
6 Dec: First flight of Silver Dart with Canadian John A.D. McCurdy at controls	Over 10 000 Quebecers leave Canada seeking jobs in U.S.	20 Apr: Naval Service Bill passed	Laurier loses national election for proposing free trade with U.S.

1900 – 1919

RECIPROCITY

"...I would say to our American neighbours.... There may be a spectacle perhaps nobler yet than the spectacle of a united continent...the spectacle of two peoples living side along a frontier nearly 4,000 miles long...with no armament one against the other, but living in harmony...with no other rivalry than a generous emulation in commerce and the arts of peace. To the Canadian people I would say that if it were possible for us to obtain such relations...[with] the powerful American republic, Canada will have rendered to old England the mother of nations, nay, to the whole British Empire, a service unequalled in its present effect, and still more in its far-reaching consequences."

— Sir Wilfrid Laurier, address in the House of Commons, 7 March 1911

(NAC C 13738)

THE CERTAIN RESULT OF A RECIPROCITY HOLE IN THE LINE FENCE

W. S. JOHNSTON & CO'Y. LIMITED, PRINTERS, TORONTO

"We are preparing to annex Canada...I am for the bill [reciprocity] because I hope to see the day when the American flag will float on every square foot of the British North American possessions clear to the North Pole."

— Champ Clark, Speaker of the House of U.S. Representatives, comment prior to the 1911 Canadian federal election

Champ Clark

"[N]ine-tenths of the people of the United States favoured annexation.... I don't care who hears me say that... Moreover I'm willing to make this proposition: You let me run for President on a platform for the annexation of Canada, in so far as this country can accomplish it, and let President Taft run against me opposing annexation — and — well, I'd carry every State in the nation."

— Champ Clark, speech, November 1911, after Laurier's defeat

▲ In 1911 the Taft administration negotiated a treaty with the Laurier government, allowing Canadian raw materials and agricultural products, including wheat, to enter American markets at lower duties. In return — this is "reciprocal trade" or "reciprocity" — Canada promised to lower its own tariff duties on American manufactured products, especially farm implements.

"[Reciprocity] means prosperity to every section of Canada. It means increased population; more trade, larger traffic for our railways; higher value for every foot of land in Canada; enlarged orders of our factories; bigger cities in short an advance all along the line."

— John W. Dafoe, editor of the *Winnipeg Free Press*

"...it was not only a dangerous experiment, but a national calamity."
— Premier Rodmond Roblin on reciprocity, quoted in the *Winnipeg Telegram*, 1911

...Everything that has occurred since reciprocity was turned down — the crop failure, the late harvest, the car shortage, the grain blockade — has only gone to confirm Saskatchewan opinion that a short haul and a handy market to the south are just the things the doctor would order. For instance, if there was reciprocity it would be a comparatively simple matter to bring the lean steer in the western states, and the unthreshed grain, which is now rotting on Saskatchewan ground, together and turn two banes into at least half a blessing.

— H. F. Gadsby, *Regina Morning Leader*, 25 April 1912

The Cry of Annexation
Ontario's sweeping verdict against reciprocity was unmistakably due to the cry of "annexation," the loyalty cry and the strong anti-American sentiment existing in this Province. This was aroused by every Conservative orator, and overshadowed altogether the economic side of the issue.

— *The Globe,* 22 September 1911

CONSERVATIVES WIN; ONTARIO IS SWEPT

Seven Members of the Cabinet Are Among the Beaten.

QUEBEC SHOWED FAITH IN LAURIER.

How the Liberal Party Fared in Various Provinces—Loyalty and Annexation Cries and Anti-American Sentiment Had Its Effect.

AMERICAN NEUTRALITY

President Wilson's Declaration of Neutrality, 19 August 1914

…The people of the United States are drawn from many nations, and chiefly from the nations now at war. It is natural and inevitable that there should be the utmost variety of sympathy and desire among them with regard to the issues and circumstances of the conflict. Some will wish one nation, others another, to succeed in the momentous struggle. It will be easy to excite passion and difficult to allay it. Those responsible for exciting it will assume a heavy responsibility, responsibility for no less a thing than that the people of the United States, whose love of their country and whose loyalty to its government should unite them as Americans all, bound in honor and affection to think first of her and her interests, may be divided in camps of hostile opinion, hot against each other, involved in the war itself in impulse and opinion if not in action.

…I venture, therefore, my fellow countrymen, to speak a solemn word of warning to you against that deepest, most subtle, most essential breach of neutrality which may spring out of partisanship, out of passionately taking sides. The United States must be neutral in fact, as well as in name, during these days that are to try men's souls.

— Woodrow Wilson, *Message to Congress*, Senate Doc. No. 566, Washington, 1914

(Library of Congress)

"The example of America must be a special example. The example of America must be the example not merely of peace because it will not fight, but of peace because peace is the healing and elevating influence of the world and strife is not. There is such a thing as a man being so right it does not need to convince others by force that it is right."

— Address of the President of the United States, Mr. Woodrow Wilson, Convention Hall, Philadelphia, Pennsylvania, 10 May 1915

"It seems so strange to be in a country that is not at war! I did not realize that until I came here how deeply Canada is at war, how normal a condition war has to come to be with us. It seems strange to go out – on the streets or to some public place – and see no khaki uniforms, no posters of appeal for recruits, no bulletin boards or war dispatches."

— L.M. Montgomery on a visit to Indiana, *Selected Journals of L. M. Montgomery, vol. II, 1910-1921*

CANADIAN COMMENTS ON AMERICAN NEUTRALITY

"America waxed richer and stronger and Canada suffered, fought and sacrificed her prosperity and her sons."

"The United States made its big mistake in allowing the Belgium tragedy… without lifting its voice in protest."
— *Montreal lawyer serving in the Canadian army overseas*

"Our big neighbour is big no longer…the true American hangs his head in shame…He is not a citizen of a nation, but belongs to a conglomeration of races undigested and indigestible; how he envies us our British citizenship and curses the spirit that he has made his country a by-word in reproach among men with red blood in their veins."
— *Major H.J. Woodside Papers, MG 30 I 11 vol.15, W.H. Gamble to Woodside, 3 February 1916*

(From J.H. Thompson & S.J. Randall, *Canada and the United States: Ambivalent Allies*, 1994)

▲ Canadians were critical of American neutrality, but criticism was muted while they prayed that the U.S. would enter the war.

For a hundred years, Canada has been at peace with the outside world. For three thousand miles along her southern border dwells a neighbour who has often been a rival in trade, and with whom Canada has had many a dispute as to fisheries and boundaries and tariff, but along...exists not a single fort, points not a single gun, watches not a single soldier.

...So why should Canada become excited over national defence? ... Guarded by a powerful nation with a Monroe Doctrine challenging the world neither to seize nor colonise in the western hemisphere. What has Canada to fear?... That Canada might some day be compelled to fight for her own existence — and fight to the death for it — never dawned on her legislators; and their unconsciousness of national peril is the profoundest testimony to the pacific intentions of the United States that could be given. It is almost treason at this era of world war to call Canada's attention to the fact that the greatest danger is not to imperial defence; it is to Canada's national defence.

Uncle Sam has been Canada's big brother, but what if when the danger came, his arms were tied in a conflict of his own? Besides, the minute Canada voluntarily enters a European war, does she not forfeit American protection under the Monroe Doctrine?

Up to the outbreak of the present war Canada has not spent $10 million a year on national defence that is — for the security of peace for a century, she has spent less than $1.50 a head per year. A year ago naval bills were rejected. Today there are few people in Canada who would not acknowledge that Canada is spending too little on defence...to the European war Canada has sent 60,000 men; and she has promised 100,000 more.

Like the United States, Canada has been inclined to sit back detached from world entanglements and perplexities. That day has passed for Canada! She must take her place and defend her place or lose her identity as a nation. The awakening has gone over Canada as like a wave. One awaits what is to come of it.

— Agnes C. Laut, *The Canadian Commonwealth*, 1915

WHO'S ABSENT?

Is it You?

1918	1919	1919	1919
Oct: Canadian steamship *Princess Sophia* sinks off Alaska coast; 343 dead	U.S. President Woodrow Wilson offers Fourteen Points as blueprint for peace	May: Treaty of Versailles signed	Prohibition begins in U.S.

1900 – 1919

THE *S.S. STEPHANO*

The German submarine U-53 paid a courtesy call to the U.S. naval base at Newport R.I. on October 10, 1916. The sailors were greeted with gifts and invitations from the American families that toured the boat. The Germans declined and left port and once outside the three mile limit fired on the British registered Stephano bound for Halifax from New York. Two U.S. navy destroyers waited as U-53 attacked the Stephano. "To have intervened would have been to violate the duty of neutrality and the Captain of the USS Balch had acted in absolute accordance with international law," said Assistant Secretary of the Navy Franklin Delano Roosevelt... — *New York Times*, 10 April 1916

"We owe our lives to the fact that the Americans were on board and that the USS Balch was there to pick us up," said Mr. Sheppard [a resident of St. John's returning from Newfoundland, where they had been taking a vacation]. "But for these two things I doubt if the submarine would have given us time to get away. The Balch took many chances in coming to our assistance, and once she passed directly between us and the submarine."

— *New York Times*, 10 October 1916

"The time will come when American democracy will need to explain..."

— *The Toronto Globe*, 11 October 1916

▲ The luxury liner *Lusitania,* was sunk by a German submarine in May 1915 on her way from New York to England, with a loss of more than 1 100 passengers and crew, including over 120 Americans. President Wilson demanded from Germany an apology, money damages, and a commitment to not use submarines again. Germany agreed to all but the latter.

"The world must be made safe for democracy."

— U.S. President Wilson, Washington, DC, 2 April 1917

"Shut Up You Sauerkraut"
Canadian veterans insulting visiting
Secretary of State as he addressed Prohibition rally

— *The Globe*, 1 March 1918

Prime Minister Borden just back after his visit to Washington described the incident where Canadian veterans sang down US Secretary of State William Jennings Bryan in Toronto in 1918, as "...no doubt a misunderstanding...but to equal Canada's record (the US) would have to place 5,500,000 men in the field."

— *The Globe*, 2 March 1918

"The malignant...anti-British figure had remained seated with his hat on as the Canadian troops marched past carrying the Union Jack"

— *Canadian Annual Review*, 5 July 1918

as a justification for continuance in the refusal to do the duty imposed on us in connection with the world war?

Unless we act with immediate decision and vigor we shall have failed in the duty demanded by humanity at large, and demanded even more clearly by the self-respect of the American Republic.

Theodore Roosevelt

Woodrow Wilson: War Message 2 April 1917

...What this will involve is clear. It will involve the utmost practicable cooperation in counsel and action with the governments now at war with Germany and, as incident to that, the extension to those governments of the most liberal financial credits, in order that our resources may so far as possible be added to theirs.... It is a fearful thing to lead this great peaceful people into war, into the most terrible and disastrous of all wars, civilization itself seeming to be in the balance. But the right is more precious than peace, and we shall fight for the things which we have always carried nearest our hearts — for democracy, for the right of those who submit to authority to have a voice of their own governments, for the rights and liberties of small nations, for a universal dominion of right by such a concert of free peoples as shall bring peace and safety to all nations and make the world itself at last free....

— 65 Congress, I Session, Senate Document No. 5

"...This is the great assembly in which all the things that are likely to disturb the peace of the world or the good understanding between nations are to be exposed to the general view, and I want to ask you if you think it was unjust, unjust to the United States, that speaking parts should be assigned to the several portions of the British Empire?... And what about Canada? Is not Canada a good neighbor? I ask you, Is not Canada more likely to agree with the United States than with Great Britain? Canada has a speaking part.... I for my part have no jealousy whatever of those five speaking parts in the assembly. Those speaking parts cannot translate themselves into five votes that can in any matter override the voice and purpose of the United States."

— President Wilson's speech on the *League of Nations* at Pueblo Colorado, 25 September 1919

AFTER THE INITIAL CELEBRATIONS marking the end of the Great War had subsided, both Canada and the United States got down to the business of business. Industry needed to retool for a peacetime economy. After a brief but severe postwar recession marked by bitter strikes, industries on both sides of the border soared. Consumer products, especially cheap automobiles and electrical appliances significantly changed North American households, cities, and economies. As business boomed trade between the two countries increased dramatically. American companies looked to Canada for energy and raw materials, and established branch plants to build cars, appliances, and other consumer goods for the protected Canadian market. As a result, the United States surpassed Britain as Canada's main trading partner in 1924 and its main source of foreign investment in 1926.

Nevertheless, the postwar boom years created many challenges for each country. With an increase in prosperity, labour organized to demand better working conditions and a fairer share of the economic pie. Membership in North American trade unions grew as a result. Women who had worked in all types of industries during the war were expected to return to their domestic roles. Many did not do so passively. A few women survived and stayed on the job. Some used their newly acquired right to vote to lobby for recognition as "Persons" and for other measures of equality. Young women "flappers" embraced the carefree social life of the "Jazz Age" while older women (and men) celebrated their victory over the "demon rum" and called for a return to strict moral values marked by the imposition of Prohibition.

Both Canada and the United States experienced Prohibition, but in somewhat different ways. While it was illegal to sell or drink alcoholic beverages in Canada, it was not illegal to produce them. Consequently, Canadian distillers made fortunes illegally selling alcohol to American gangsters, smuggling the product across our long, undefended border. Out of Prohibition came such memorable characters and symbols as Elliot Ness and Al Capone, rum-runners and speakeasies. Unfortunately, along with the rise of organized crime, the 1920s also witnessed the rise of racial intolerance epitomized by the Ku Klux Klan which made inroads into both Ontario and Alberta.

The industrial boom of the 1920s fuelled a dramatic rise in the stock market. Just before the end of the decade, the great prosperity came to an end in a resounding Stock Market Crash which signalled the beginning of a decade known as the Great Depression.

HALIBUT TREATY

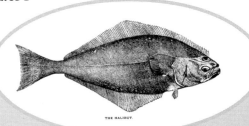

THE HALIBUT.

His Ex. [the Governor General] spoke of the Treaty, said it had given him pleasure to see it accomplished.... I told His Ex. I was sure it was right to remove any badge of 'colonialism'

— Diary of Mackenzie King, 2 March 1923

▲ King insisted that a Canadian minister alone should sign the treaty on behalf of Canada, without the participation of the British ambassador. Ernest Lapointe, Minister of Marine and Fisheries, signed for Canada.

TREATY FOR THE PROTECTION OF THE PACIFIC HALIBUT
2 March 1923

Article I

The nationals and inhabitants and the fishing vessels and boats, of the Dominion of Canada and of the United States, respectively, are hereby prohibited from fishing for halibut (Hippoglossus) both in the territorial waters and in the high seas off the western coast of the Dominion of Canada and of the United States, including Bering Sea, from the 16th day of November next after the date of the exchange of ratifications of this Convention, to the 15th day of the following February, both days inclusive, and within the same period yearly thereafter, provided that upon the recommendation of the International Fisheries Commission hereinafter described this close season may be modified or suspended at any time after the expiration of three such seasons, by a special agreement concluded and duly ratified by the High Contracting Parties....

Article II

Every national or inhabitant, vessel or boat of the Dominion of Canada or of the United States engaged in halibut fishing in violation of preceding Article may be seized except within the jurisdiction of the other Party by the duly authorized officers of either High Contracting Party and detained by the officers making such seizure — and delivered as soon as practicable to an authorized official of the country to which such person, vessel or boat belongs, at the nearest point to the place of seizure, or elsewhere, as may be mutually agreed upon....

(Sgd.) ERNEST LAPOINTE
(Sgd.) CHARLES EVANS HUGHES

▲ The Halibut Treaty was an agreement between Canada and the U.S. on fishing rights in the North Pacific ocean. Britain wanted to sign this agreement with the U.S. along with Canada, but PM Mackenzie King argued that the matter was only between Canada and the U.S., and that Britain would have no business in being there. On 2 March 1923, this treaty became the first foreign treaty independently negotiated and signed by the Canadian government.

FISHERIES CONVENTION SIGNED AT WASHINGTON

Canada and U.S. Agree Upon Closed Season for Halibut Fishing in North Pacific

Hoped That Industry Which Is Being Rapidly Depleted Will Be Prolonged

▲ Meighen campaign poster.

▶ Higher Canadian tariffs and demand for consumer goods led major American companies to set up branch plants in Canada during the early 1900s. This allowed for cheaper access to markets in Canada and the British Commonwealth.

THE ECONOMY

CANADIAN EXPORTS IN SELECTED YEARS 1901 – 1931 (in millions of dollars)			
Year	Canadian exports to Britain	Canadian exports to the U.S.	Canadian exports to other countries
1901	101	68	26
1911	149	104	37
1921	403	542	265
1931	220	240	140

(Historical Atlas of Canada, Volume III)

▲ In 1921, for the first time in its history, Canada exports more goods (excluding gold) to the United States than to Great Britain.

The steady influx of the United States business firms into Canada mainly by the establishment of branches in Ontario, is having a considerable effect on commercial real estate.... Canadians have always welcomed the establishment of American branch plants here...in 1918 34% of the securities of our manufacturing companies were owned in the United States, according to the Dominion Bureau of Statistics...about 600 recognised branches of the United States manufacturing companies, there are several hundred, "so called Canadian," plants that are in reality controlled from New York, Chicago, or other large financial centres.... So much constructive enterprise...the outlook is bright for solid progress all around.

— "The American Influx," *The Mail and Empire*, March 1922

AMERICANIZATION OF CANADIAN CULTURE

"Take the most potent influence at work on the popular mind, our journalism....[N]ot only is the Canadian newspaper built on American lines...it is crammed with American boilerplate of all kinds, American illustration, American comic supplements.... Another potent influence for bringing Canada into spiritual subjection to the United states is the moving picture show. The films are made for American audiences, naturally, to suit their tastes. Then they come to Canada. We originate none practically."

— Archibald MacMechan (1862–1933), Canadian critic and academic, 1920

▼ In the 1920s, Canadians listened to mostly American radio. By 1928, public concern with the "Americanization" of Canadian culture through radio led to the formation of the Canadian Broadcasting Corporation in 1932.

~ TOTAL RADIO STATION POWER OUTPUT, 1920s ~
Canada: 50 kilowatts
United States: 6 800 kilowatts

(ZUMA Movie Stills Library/PHOTOPLAY, 1922)

▲ The influence of the American "flapper look" on women in the streets of Toronto.

(Glenbow Archives NC-6-11966c)

▲ Most movies watched by Canadians in the 1920s were made in Hollywood, with emphasis on American culture and heroes. If Canadians appeared in film, they were usually mounties or French lumberjacks.

(WM NA66-1691)

PROHIBITION

THE UNITED STATES CONSTITUTION
18th Amendment (1919)

Section 1. After one year from the ratification of this article the man-ufacture, sale, or transportation of intoxicating liquors within, the importation thereof into, or the exportation thereof from the United States and all territory subject to the jurisdiction thereof for beverage purposes is hereby prohibited.

Section 2. The Congress and the several states shall have concurrent power to enforce this article by appropriate legislation.

Section 3. This article shall be inoperative unless it shall have been ratified as an amendment to the Constitution by the legislatures of the several states, as provided in the Constitution, within seven years from the date of the submission hereof to the states by the Congress.

◄ By constitutional amendment, the U.S. was under even stricte prohibition than was Canada — from 1920-33 the manufacture sale, and transportation of all alcohol were forbidden in the U.S Liquor legally produced in or imported into Canada was exported legally under Canadian law to its "dry" neighbour.

▲ Woman demonstrating how young women smuggled liquor on a Windsor-Detroit ferry. In 1924, $30 million of Canadian liquor was shipped to the U.S. via the Detroit River and the Great Lakes. The estimated value in the U.S. was $100 million. It was estimated that up to 25% of the Windsor population was involved in some form of smuggling.

(*Walkerville Times*)

▲ Smugglers delivered illegal shipments of alcohol to their U.S. customers any way they could. One way was to use old cars or trucks called "flivvers," in case they went through the ice. In some cases both vehicle and smug-gler went through the ice. In 1928, 28 bodies were fished out of the Detroit River and Lake Erie south of Amherstburg, Ontario.

THE SINKING OF THE *I'M ALONE*

◄ The crew of *I'm Alone* after its sinking. The *I'm Alone*, flying a Canadian flag, was sunk by the U.S. Coast Guard in the Gulf of Mexico, resulting in the death of one crew member. The Canadian Government sued the U.S. for $365 000 and the ensuing legal battle brought world-wide attention.

Seizure of Diplomatic Liquor Creates Incident

...The Coast Guard Commandant called the *I'm Alone* a "notorious rum runner" and explained that the U.S. cutter Walcott had ordered the two-master to halt for inspection. Instead of stopping, the *I'm Alone* turned and fled. Cornered by other U.S. craft 24 hours later on the high seas, the *I'm Alone* was sent down by gunfire. One man was lost. The rest of the crew, in irons, were carried to New Orleans. The *I'm Alone's* skipper said his schooner was "anchored 14 to 15 miles offshore" and he did not heave to because he did not think the U.S. had jurisdiction. His ship, he figured, went down 225 miles offshore in a heavy sea under 120 U.S. shots. — *Time* Magazine, 1 April 1929

Claim of the British Ship "I'm Alone" v. United States
(1935)
REPORTS OF THE COMMISSIONERS

The *I'm Alone*, a British ship of Canadian registry, but de facto owned, controlled and managed by a group of American citi-zens engaged in smuggling liquor into the United States, was sunk on the high seas in the Gulf of Mexico by a United States coast guard patrol boat, with the loss of one member of the *I'm Alone's* crew, on March 22, 1929...

Held, that under the Convention of Jan. 23, 1924, between the United States and Great Britain to prevent the smuggling of intoxicating liquors into the United States...that the admitted-ly intentional sinking of the vessel was not justified by anything in the Convention or by any principle of international law.

Held further, that no compensation ought to be paid in respect of the loss of the ship or cargo, but that the United States ought to apologize to Canada and pay that Government the sum of $25,000 as a material amend, and also pay the additional sum of $26,666.50 for the benefit of the captain and crew of the *I'm Alone*, none of whom was a party to the illegal conspiracy to smuggle liquor into the United States and sell the same there.

1927
18 Feb: U.S. and Canada establish diplomatic relations independently of Great Britain

1927
7 Aug: Peace Bridge between U.S. and Canada dedicated

1929
29 Oct: Montreal and Toronto stock markets suffer worst crash in Canadian history

1929
Jan 2: U.S. and Canada reach agreement to preserve Niagara Falls

THE AMERICAN INFLUENCE

"…Every social organism must have a head, but every individual in the organism must live its own free life. That is true democracy. But of course you don't understand democracy, you Canadians."

"Aha! There you are! You Americans are the most insular of all the great peoples of the world. You know nothing of other people. You know only your own history and not even that correctly, your own geography, and your own political science. You know nothing of Canada. You don't know, for instance, that the purest form of democracy on this American continent lies outside the bounds of the U. S. A."

"In Canada?" she asked scornfully. "By the way, how many Canadians are there?"…

— Ralph Connor, *The Sky Pilot*, 1921

▲ Canadian novels were in international demand in the 1920s and desired for Hollywood scripts. Ralph Connor was one of the five best-selling Canadian authors of all time: sales of his novel *The Sky Pilot* exceeded one million copies in the U.S. Hollywood bought the novel and de-Canadianized it. The only Canadian reference in the entire movie is that the Sky Pilot comes from Montreal.

Canadian and American History

One of the curious features of our present-day Universities…is the fact that the history taught in them is predominantly the history of England and Europe, and that the students are encouraged directly or indirectly to despise the history of their own country and of the continent of which it forms a part. Anyone who knows the inside of a Canadian University is familiar with the slightly amused condescension with which the genteel members of its history department greet the suggestion from some outer barbarian that the most important history for Canadians to study is Canadian history and that the next most important is American history, because the United States forms part of the same continent and the same western world as ourselves…. Both distance and poverty make it impossible for us to keep in real touch with Europe, and it is only a snobbish colonialism which prevents our historians from recognising the fact and acting accordingly. We must cease to gaze wistfully across the ocean and we must turn our energies to the vast unexplored fields which lie all around us…

— Frank H. Underhill, *Canadian Forum*, June 1928

"The boundary between Canada and the United States is a typically human creation; it is physically invisible, geographically illogical, militarily indefensible, and emotionally inescapable."

— Hugh L. Keenleyside, Canadian Diplomat, 1929

STOCK MARKET CRASH OF 1929

Stock prices virtually collapsed yesterday, swept downward with gigantic losses in the most disastrous trading day in the stock market's history. Billions of dollars in open market values were wiped out as prices crumbled under the pressure of liquidation of securities which had to be sold at any price…. Efforts to estimate yesterday's market losses in dollars are futile because of the vast number of securities quoted over the counter and on out-of-town exchanges on which no calculations are possible. However, it was estimated that 880 issues, on the New York Stock Exchange, lost between $8,000,000,000 and $9,000,000,000 yesterday…. Groups of men, with here and there a woman, stood about inverted glass bowls all over the city yesterday watching spools of ticker tape unwind and as the tenuous paper with its cryptic numerals grew longer at their feet their fortunes shrank. Others sat stolidly on tilted chairs in the customers' rooms of brokerage houses and watched a motion picture of waning wealth as the day's quotations moved silently across a screen….

— *New York Times*, 30 October 1929

Record for All Time Is Set by Wall Street In Frenzy of Selling

Most Disastrous Decline in History of New York Stock Exchange Sees 12,894,650 Shares Change Hand —Total of 974 Separate Issues Handled—Thousands of Accounts Wiped Out Before Leading Bankers Combine to Halt Slump—Losses Reported to Reach Billions of Dollars

FINANCIAL LEADERS IN CONFERENCE ISSUE REASSURING STATEMENT

Securities Markets of Country Feel Effects of Downward Movement—Chicago Prices Break in Record Day's Trading of 1,220,000 Shares—London Spends Nervous Day Watching Events Across Atlantic

(The Globe, 24 October 1929)

CRASH IN NEW YORK ROCKS SHARE PRICES IN TORONTO MARKETS

Rush of Orders Demoralizes Communications for a Time

MINES SHARES AFFECTED

Vigorous Upswing Late in Day—Montreal Exchange Has Record Day

Unable to withstand the sudden and terrific pressure of record-breaking liquidation, prices on the Toronto and Montreal Stock Exchanges collapsed yesterday in a market which made financial history. Vigorous Upturn.

Almost as rapidly as it had declined, the stock market turned vigorously upward in the afternoon, and many of the day's extreme declines at Toronto and Montreal were reduced by as much as 50 per cent.

Equally encouraging was the fact that the Standard Stock and Mining Exchange not only withstood the effect of selling on other m...

(The Globe, Toronto, 24 October 1929)

1930 - 1939

1930
17 June: Smoot-Hawley Tariff Act

1930
18 June: Canadian tariff increased

1931
Dec: 25 countries retaliate against American protectionism and tariff policy

THE 1930S WAS a decade of worldwide suffering caused by devastating economic conditions. The manic speculation that had led to the Stock Market Crash in October 1929 signalled the beginning of a decade-long Great Depression.

Since the social consequences on both sides of the border were very similar, the cultural responses tended to be the same. Hollywood created a fantasy world of opulence and escapism through extravagant musicals and fluffy romances. Big band jazz, afternoon soap operas, and vaudeville comedians dominated the radio airwaves on both sides of the border. The lives of a few special children — movie star Shirley Temple, Canada's Dionne quintuplets, and the royal princesses, Elizabeth and Margaret — became the focus of attention across North America.

The different political responses within each country to the challenges of the Depression illustrate differences in values and in political leadership. In Canada, the old-line parties clung to power despite offering little real change. Consequently, more radical responses to the dire economic and social circumstances found expression in the creation of new political parties such as the Co-operative Commonwealth Federation (CCF), Social Credit, and, in Quebec, the Union Nationale. In the United States, established political parties either refused to change and, like Hoover's Republicans, lost power; or, like the Democrats, were forced to change by the rise of new leaders such as Huey Long in Louisiana and Franklin Delano Roosevelt nationally. In the United States, the very survival of democracy lay in its ability to find solutions to the substantial problems of the era and, in Canada, in the willingness of the people to believe that the system would eventually reward the faith that was placed in it. The New Deal solutions implemented by President Roosevelt after his election in 1932 set the stage. They were so popular that even Canada's Conservative Prime Minister, R. B. Bennett, campaigned for re-election on a "New Deal" platform. However, it was "too little too late," and Mackenzie King's Liberals were returned to power, despite offering no real solutions of their own.

Economic devastation in Europe led to civil wars, the destruction of democracies, and the rise of Fascism in Italy and Portugal in the 1920s and in Germany and Spain during the 1930s. As Nazi Germany ride roughshod over Poland in September of 1939 and began the takeover of most of Europe, Canadians once again decided to support Britain in war. As they had done in 1914, the Americans chose isolation, although Roosevelt later found ways to supply Canada and Britain with much-needed weapons, supplies, and credit, despite Congress' demands for neutrality.

SMOOT-HAWLEY TARIFF ACT OF 1930

Impact of Smoot-Hawley on U.S. Economy GDP and Exports, 1929-1933						
Year	Nominal GDP	Real GDP	Nominal Net Exports	Real Net Exports	Nominal Exports	Real Exports
1929	$103.1	$103.1	$0.4	$0.3	$5.9	$5.9
1930	$90.4	$93.3	$0.3	$0.0	$4.4	$4.9
1931	$75.8	$86.1	$0.0	-$0.4	$2.9	$4.1
1932	$58.0	$74.7	$0.0	-$0.3	$2.0	$3.3
1933	$55.6	$73.2	$0.1	-$0.4	$2.0	$3.3

▲ U.S. legislation raised import duties by almost 60%, substantially higher than tariffs anywhere else in the world, triggering comparable tariff increases by U.S. trading partners, including Canada.

"[T]he countervailing duties [are] designed to give a practical illustration to the United States of the desire of Canada to trade at all times on fair and equal terms. For the present we raise the duties on these selected commodities to the level applied against Canadian exports of the same commodities by other countries, but at the same time we tell our neighbour we are ready in the future to consider trade on a reciprocal basis."
— Mackenzie King, 1930

"How many thousands of American workmen are living on Canadian money today? They've got the jobs and we've got the soup kitchens? I will not beg of any country to buy our goods. I will make [tariffs] fight for you. I will use them to blast a way into markets that have been closed…"

— R.B. Bennett, Conservative candidate, campaign speech, July 1930

▲ As Smoot-Hawley neared passage, King came under intense pressure to retaliate. In May 1930 Canada imposed so-called countervailing duties on several imports from the U.S. at levels charged by the U.S. Bennett won the election and pushed through the Canadian Parliament further tariff increases.

CANADA-U.S. TRADE AGREEMENT

OFFICIAL STATEMENTS AT SIGNING OF PACT

(Underwood & Underwood/NAC C 031017)

▲ PM King, FDR, and Cordell Hull sign the reciprocal trade agreement in Washington, 15 November 1935. The treaty granted Canada lower rates or other concessions on 2/3 of its exports by volume to the U.S. The U.S., in turn, received concessions on 3/4 of its dutiable exports to Canada.

PRESIDENT ROOSEVELT.
…The signing of this agreement marks the reversal of the trend of the last two decades toward undue and unnecessary trade barriers between our two countries. I am confident that this constructive step will contribute greatly to the economic recovery of both the United States and Canada.

PRIME MINISTER KING.
…I believe with you that the signature of this agreement is witness of the joint intention of the governments of the United States and Canada to give rapid affect to our policies in a practical manner. At last our formal trade relations have been brought into harmony with the underlying realities of public and private friendship between our two peoples. The agreement will, I am confident, confer substantial benefits alike on the producers and consumers of both countries, while safeguarding with great care every essential interest.

— *The New York Times*, 16 November 1935

ROOSEVELT VISITS CANADA

(NAC C 16768)

▸ Mackenzie King and U.S. President Franklin D. Roosevelt, 31 July 1936, during Roosevelt's visit to Quebec City — the first time a U.S. President had ever visited Canada.

> *"We are fortunate both in our neighbours and in our lack of neighbours."*
>
> — PM Mackenzie King, Ottawa, 1936

"A few days ago a whisper, fortunately untrue, raced 'round the world that armies standing over against each other in unhappy array were about to be set in motion. In a few short hours the effect of that whisper had been registered in Montreal and New York, in Ottawa and in Washington, in Toronto and in Chicago, in Vancouver and in San Francisco.... Happily, you and we, in friendship and in entire understanding, can look clear-eyed at these possibilities, resolving to leave no pathway unexplored, no technique undeveloped which may, if our hopes are realized, contribute to the peace of the world. Even if those hopes are disappointed, we can assure each other that this hemisphere at least shall remain a strong citadel wherein civilization can flourish unimpaired.... The Dominion of Canada is part of the sisterhood of the British Empire. I give to you assurance that the people of the United States will not stand idly by if domination of Canadian soil is threatened by any other Empire."

— FDR's Address at Queen's University, Kingston, Ontario, 18 August 1938

British, American and Other Foreign Capital Investment in Canada, 1920-1939 (millions of dollars)				
Year	United Kingdom	United States	Other	Total
1920	2,577.3	2,128.2	164.6	4,870.1
1925	2,345.7	3,219.2	149.2	5,714.1
1926*	2,591.5	3,108.8	63.3	5,763.6
1933	2,682.8	4,491.7	190.0	7,364.5
1935	2,729.3	4,044.6	123.6	6,897.5
1939	2,475.9	4,151.4	286.0	6,913.3

* Figures from 1926 to 1939 are official estimates by the Dominion Bureau of Statistics

> *"We are not in the same boat, but we are pretty much in the same waters."*
>
> — PM Arthur Meighen, address on Can-U.S. relations, 1937

"That long frontier from the Atlantic to the Pacific oceans, guarded only by neighbourly respect and honorable obligations, is an example to every country and a pattern for the future of the world."

— Winston Churchill, Prime Minister of Great Britain, speech given at Canada Club, London, England, 1939

CROSS-BORDER LABOUR UNIONS

...Why did the workers seek a union here? Why did so many join in such a short time? Because there was a festering sore here that had grown as a result of the vicious attitude of the corporation towards its employees... The so-called shop representation plan was a complete failure. The company laid off men and hired them as they saw fit. I have the records in the office. They show where men who worked 27 and 30 years for the company were laid off and had to go on relief. Men saw there was no protection, no security. That was the ground in which the seeds of an organization like ours, once planted, struck deep roots and spread fast...

— *The Toronto Star*, 9 April 1937

CHARTER
International Union United Automobile Workers of America Affiliated with the American Federation of Labour

...[T]his Charter [is granted] for the establishment and future maintenance of a Local Union at Windsor, Ontario, Canada, to be known as Local Union No. 195 of International Union, United Automobile Workers of America.
...That the said Union forever and under any circumstances shall be subordinate to and comply with all the requirements of the constitution, by-laws and general laws or other laws of the International Union, United Automobile Workers of America...
That said Union shall...be guided and controlled by all acts and decisions of the International Union, United Automobile Workers of America... — Upton Sinclair

---

APPLICATION FORM
for membership to
The Auto Workers' Industrial Union
OF THE BORDER CITIES

I believe in an Industrial Union for Automobile Workers as the only effective organization for defending and fighting for the interests of the workers in the Auto industry.

Name ....
Address ....
Age .... Sex ....
Department ....

N.B. Mail this card together with One Dollar ($1.00) as initiation, to the undersigned, who will notify you of the meeting date.

Secretary,
Devonshire Road, Walkerville, Ont.

(Excerpt from The Worker, 14 July 1928/Public Archives of Canada)

▸ The United Automobile Workers of Canada was founded as an affiliate of the American UAW in 1937, winning its first concessions from General Motors during the Oshawa Strike.

1940 - 1949

1940	1941	1941
Ogdensburg Agreement establishes Joint Board on Defence	Canadian troops surrender British Colony of Hong Kong to Japanese	20 Apr: Hyde Park Declaration issued

As a new decade dawned, Canadian troops found themselves back in Britain waiting for their marching orders. Americans were determined to remain isolated despite the urgings of President Roosevelt to support the war. He was able to provide Canada and her allies some assistance through programs such as Lend-Lease and the Ogdensburg and Hyde Park agreements. However, it took the Japanese attack on the American naval base at Pearl Harbor to force the U.S. into war. The relationship between Canada and the U.S. strengthened as both countries worked to defeat the Axis powers. Together, we built the Alaska-Canadian Highway; created the combined force of Special Operatives, the Devil's Brigade; participated in the D-Day invasion of Normandy; and worked through the Manhattan Project to build the first atomic bomb. The combined efforts of the Allies led to the total defeat of Nazi Germany in May 1945. In August 1945, Japan surrendered after the nuclear destruction of Hiroshima and Nagasaki.

Once the Axis had been defeated, Canadian and American diplomats helped found the United Nations, with the aim of promoting peace, prosperity, security, and cooperation in the world. A cornerstone of this effort was the Universal Declaration of Human Rights written in 1948 by a Canadian, John Humphrey.

Although the hostilities had ceased, new and dramatic tensions between communist Soviet Union and the West escalated into the Cold War. When it was revealed by a Russian cipher clerk in Ottawa that Soviet spies were operating in Canada and the U.S., an almost paranoiac atmosphere gripped the Americans. Led by Senator Joe McCarthy and the House Un-American Activities Committee, the FBI and other law enforcement agencies began to identify and disrupt the lives of socialists and communists from all walks of American life. Canada was not immune to such actions as evidenced by the jailing, amongst others, of our only elected Communist MP, Fred Rose. Canada and the United States played an integral role in the creation of NATO, a defensive military alliance against the Soviet Bloc.

Life in the postwar world generated many social, cultural, and demographic changes. Peacetime production in both Canada and the U.S. expanded to meet demands for consumer goods, especially automobiles and housing, that had been pent up for over 15 years. Young men and women who had delayed marriage and families during the Depression and the war were getting married and having children in record numbers. The postwar baby boom and the automobile led to the rapid expansion of cities and the rise of suburbs. This new generation of "Baby Boomers" were also the first to grow up with television.

JOINT DEFENCE

(NAC C 005767)

▲ First Meeting of the Canada-United States Permanent Joint Board on Defence, Ottawa, 26 August 1940.

To the Congress:

I transmit herewith for the information of the Congress notes exchanged between the British Ambassador at Washington and the Secretary of State...under which this Government has acquired the right to lease naval and air bases in Newfoundland, and in the islands of Bermuda, the Bahamas, Jamaica, St. Lucia, Trinidad, and Antigua, and in British Guiana; also a copy of an opinion of the Attorney General dated August 27, 1940, regarding my authority to consummate this arrangement.

The right to bases in Newfoundland and Bermuda are gifts — generously given and gladly received. The other bases mentioned have been acquired in exchange for 50 of our over-age destroyers.

This is not inconsistent in any sense with our status of peace. Still less is it a threat against any nation. It is an epochal and far-reaching act of preparation for continental defense in the face of grave danger....

The value to the Western Hemisphere of these outposts of security is beyond calculation.... Their consequent importance in hemispheric defense is obvious. For these reasons I have taken advantage of the present opportunity to acquire them.

— Franklin D. Roosevelt, message to Congress, 3 September 1940

▲ In September 1940 the U.S. transferred 50 over-age destroyers to the Royal Navy in return for long-term (99 year) leases on British naval bases in the Eastern Atlantic. The Lend-Lease Act of 1941 gave Roosevelt virtually unlimited authority to direct material aid such as ammunition, tanks, airplanes, and food to the war effort in Europe. This program brought the U.S. one step closer to direct involvement.

"The United States should loan what articles were needed, as a man would loan his garden hose to help his neighbor put out a fire without reference to payment, but with the expectation that the hose itself would be returned."

— Franklin D. Roosevelt, 17 December 1941

1941
7 Dec: Japan launches surprise attack on Pearl Harbor

1942
21 Nov: Alaska Highway across Canada formally opens

1944
6 June: Canadian troops storm Juno Beach on D-Day

1944
11 Sept: Roosevelt and Churchill meet in Canada at second Quebec Conference

HYDE PARK DECLARATION, 1941

...It was agreed as a general principle that in mobilizing the resources of this continent each country should provide the other with the defence articles which it is best able to produce, and, above all, produce quickly, and that production programs should be co-ordinated to this end.

While Canada has expanded its productive capacity manifold since the beginning of the war, there are still numerous defence articles which it must obtain in the United States, and purchases of this character by Canada will be even greater in the coming year than in the past. On the other hand, there is existing and potential capacity in Canada for the speedy production of certain kinds of munitions, strategic materials, aluminum, and ships, which are urgently required by the United States for its own purposes.

While exact estimates cannot yet be made, it is hoped that during the next twelve months Canada can supply the United States with between $200,000,000 and $300,000,000 worth of such defence articles. This sum is a small fraction of the total defence program of the United States, but many of the articles to be provided are of vital importance. In addition, it is of great importance to the economic and financial relations between the two countries that payment by the United States for these supplies will materially assist Canada in meeting part of the cost of Canadian defence purchases in the United States....

THE U.S. ENTERS THE WAR

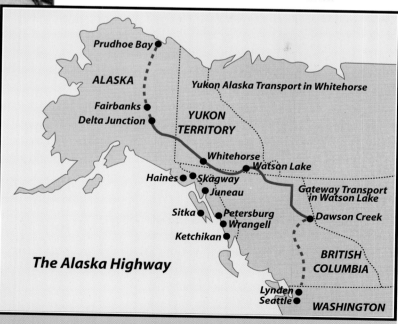

▲ Official checking documents. Japanese Canadians were relocated to camps in the British Columbia interior.

(NAC PA 112539)

▲ Students at St. Mary's School in Vancouver rehearsing for a Japanese attack. In December 1941, the Japanese attacked the U.S. naval base at Pearl Harbor in Hawaii, forcing America's entry into WW II. The closest Canada came to the war was a Japanese U-boat shelling at Estevan Point on Vancouver Island.

▶ Thousands of American servicemen flooded Alberta, British Columbia, and the Yukon to build the Alaska Highway, meant to transport troops north if the Japanese attacked again. The Highway was completed in six months and officially opened on 20 November 1942.

A road 1,600 miles long, through virgin wilderness, across terrain considered some of the roughest and most inaccessible in the world, was to be built.... And the army had a definite plan. It was to tackle the construction of the road from several points simultaneously. Ten thousand soldiers, white and negro, were to be used. These, separated into various gangs, would blast its stretch of route, eventually they would meet. They would connect. The road would be there....

— Gertrude Baskine, *Hitch-Hiking the Alaska Highway*, 1944

The Alaska Highway

Map labels: Prudhoe Bay, ALASKA, Fairbanks, Delta Junction, Yukon Alaska Transport in Whitehorse, YUKON TERRITORY, Whitehorse, Watson Lake, Haines, Skagway, Juneau, Gateway Transport in Watson Lake, Sitka, Petersburg, Wrangell, Dawson Creek, Ketchikan, BRITISH COLUMBIA, Lynden, Seattle, WASHINGTON

"During the past year we have heard much about the building of the Alaska highway.... Canadians must not forget that it is being built and will be maintained throughout the war by the United States with United States money...."

— Georges Black (Yukon), House of Commons debates, 1943

THE MANHATTAN PROJECT

Canada Must Be Uranium Ally or Else, Says N.Y.

The U.S. must have uranium and plenty of it, if it will deliver the devastation claimed at Hiroshima. Canada will serve its own best interest as well as ours by making uranium in ample quantity to us and by making it not available to other nations... As for uranium, Canada should make itself our exclusive ally. If it won't do so, well, we now have the jump on the rest of the world as regards manufacture and manipulation of atom bombs and enough patriotic Americans could probably...see to it that Canada does the right thing by us and by itself with its uranium.

— *New York Daily News*, 8 August 1945

▶ In 1946, Winnipeg-born scientist Louis Slotin performed a risky experiment called "tickling the dragon's tail," in which two globes of plutonium were brought together until separated only by a screwdriver. The globes touched and set off a nuclear chain reaction. Slotkin pushed the globes apart with his bare hands to stop the reaction, saving seven American co-workers in the room but subjecting himself to a lethal dose of the radiation. Within a week he died an excruciating death.

◀ The "Manhattan Project" was the code name for the U.S. program to develop the atomic bomb during WW II. Canadian technology and uranium were vital factors in the program. While Canada was the first nation with nuclear capacity to renounce the development of its own nuclear weapons, it has contributed to nuclear proliferation in many ways, mainly through uranium exports and the sale of Candu reactors.

....

"How strange it is that I should find myself at the very centre of the problem through Canada possessing uranium, having contributed to the production of the bomb, being recognized as one of the three countries to hold most of the secrets."

— Mackenzie King, diary, 11 October 1945

(Wash. NAC C-023269)

▲ President Harry Truman, British PM Clement Atlee, and PM Mackenzie King meet on-board the U.S. Coast Guard ship *Sequoia* in November 1945, three months after the atomic bomb had been dropped on Japan, to discuss atomic energy.

"1. We recognize that the application of recent scientific discoveries to the methods and practice of war has placed at the disposal of mankind means of destruction hitherto unknown, against which there can be no adequate military defense, and in the employment of which no single nation can in fact have a monopoly.

2. ...the responsibility for devising means to ensure that the new discoveries shall be used for the benefit of mankind, instead of as a means of destruction, rests not on our nations alone, but upon the whole civilized world....we have...met together to consider the possibility of international action:

(a) To prevent the use of atomic energy for destructive purposes.

(b) To promote the use of recent and future advances in scientific knowledge, particularly in the utilization of atomic energy, for peaceful and humanitarian ends."...

— Harry S. Truman (with British PM Atlee and PM Mackenzie King), The President's News Conference following the signing of a Joint Declaration on Atomic Energy, 15 November 1945

Is the United States unduly aggressive? the very intimacy, informality and friendliness of the relationship led them to consider us not as a foreign nation at all, but as one of themselves...flattering but it perplexed them...when we show an impatience at being ignored and an irritation at being treated as something less than an independent State.... When we are dealing with such a powerful neighbour, we have to avoid the twin dangers of subservience and truculent touchiness. We succumb to the former when we take everything lying down, and to the latter when we rush to the State Department with a note every time some Congressman makes a stupid statement about Canada, or some documentary movie about the war forgets to mention Canada....

— Lester Pearson, minister-counsellor at the Canadian Legation, comment in memorandum "United States Policy Towards Canada," March 1944

SAN FRANCISCO CONFERENCE

▶ Nearly 300 delegates representing 50 nations met at the San Francisco Conference on 25 April 1945 to reach agreement on an international organization to keep peace in the postwar world. The most important document to come out of the Conference was the Charter of the United Nations.

"American policy or...American tactics in this conference are similar to British.... There does not seem to be much attempt to understand the viewpoint of the smaller nations or to produce reasoned arguments to meet their objections."

— Charles Ritchie, senior official, Department of External Affairs, from his diary of the San Francisco Conference, cited in his book, *The Siren Years: A Canadian Diplomat Abroad, 1937-194...*

D-DAY

> *"Canada and the United States have reached the point where we can no longer think of each other as 'foreign' countries."*
>
> — Harry S. Truman, U.S. president, address, joint sitting of the Canadian Senate and House of Commons, 11 June 1947

(NAC PA 135964)

▸ 6 June 1944: soldiers from the Allied nations invaded Normandy, France to begin its liberation from Nazism. Canadians and Americans joined their British counterparts on this day to begin the steady push to eliminate Fascism from Western Europe. Canada's responsibility that day was Juno Beach, one of the five assigned invasion beaches; the United States was responsible for two beaches – Utah and Omaha.

COLD WAR ESPIONAGE

▸ Cipher clerk Igor Gouzenko defected from the USSR Embassy in September 1945 with more than 100 secret documents, detailing the workings of a major Soviet spy ring in Canada, with tentacles reaching into the Department of External Affairs code room, the British High Commissioner's Office, and the Chalk River nuclear facility. WW II had just ended and the Soviet Union and Canada were supposed to be allies. Canadian PM Mackenzie King was trying to maintain good relations with Stalin, and ignored Gouzenko. Ottawa finally listened, resulting in 20 espionage trials and nine convictions.

adverse opinions held by the Soviet inspectors with regard to the American organization in 1944. Kulakov informed Ouzenko that although the Canadian organization was closely knit and well operated and most productive, that there were, of course, more agents in the United States and that he had learned in Moscow that an Assistant of Stettinius, then the United States Secretary of State, was a Soviet spy. Guzenko pointed out that this information would necessarily have come to Kulakov's attention prior to May 17, 1945, because Kulakov left Moscow for the United States and Canada on that date. He stated that he did not ask for the name of this individual because Kulakov would have suspected his motives, since it involved an individual who was not being run by Colonel Zabotin.

Guzenko pointed out that the Soviets were frantic to obtain the secrets of the atomic bomb and that an incident had been reported in the press recently which appeared to him to have been inspired by a Soviet agent. This Soviet agent might not necessarily be the same one to whom Kulakov referred, but on the other hand, it had all the earmarks of the technique used by Soviet political espionage agents. He referred specifically to the announcement made in London by Stettinius that the atomic bomb should be turned over to the Security Council of the United Nations. Guzenko suggested that if the Bureau [...] s that this statement be made, the [...] agent, if not the Assistant to

Guzenko stated that the Soviets before the use of the atomic bomb were confident that within ten years their military potential would enable them to conquer the world. Since the atomic bomb has been used by the United States, they have set their calendar ahead and have instructed all espionage agents to make the obtaining of the complete construction plans of the bomb itself the No. 1 espionage project. They have issued instructions that this information should be obtained by the end of this year, 1945. Guzenko stated that the last message received at the Embassy from Moscow before he left on September 5, 1945, was stressing the necessity for obtaining the atomic bomb before the end of this year.

NORTH ATLANTIC TREATY ORGANISATION (NATO)

"Well, the fear of subversive communism allied to the soviet might is in fact the mainspring of the development…to this North Atlantic Treaty Pact. Hon. Members know what those developments were…

The treaty, if signed, will bring together in alliance against war the free nations of the North Atlantic community which share a common heritage, a common civilization, a common belief in the purposes and principles of the charter of the United Nations and a common desire to live in peace with all peoples and all governments….

This treaty is to be far more than an old-fashioned military alliance. It is based on the common belief of the north Atlantic nations in the values and virtues of our Christian civilization. It is based on our common determination to strengthen our free institutions and to promote conditions of stability and well-being. It is based on the belief that we have in our collective manpower, in our collective natural resources, in our collective industrial potential and industrial know-how, that which would make us a very formidable enemy for any possible aggressor to attack.

This is, of course, a serious step for this young nation, but I think it is a step that will implement the desire of all the Canadian people that civilized Christian nations should at some time abandon trial by might for the rule of law."

— Louis St. Laurent, speech, House of Commons, 28 March 1949

Louis St. Laurent

(NAC C 10461)

> *"Our frontier… has long been undefended, but realists have observed that the disparity of population has made armaments for one country futile and for the other superfluous."*
>
> — Vincent Massey, Governor General of Canada, on being Canadian, 1948

1950 - 1959

1950	1951	1955
Canada joins UN contingent in Korean War	The Massey Commission	12 Apr: Ottawa moves to produce and distribute a polio vaccine after successful trials in U.S.

THE FIFTIES USHERED IN an unprecedented decade of rapid and sustained economic growth built on consumerism. Canada experienced a doubling of total national output from $18.4 to $36.8 billion while the U.S. saw its GNP grow 57% to reach $600 billion by the decade's end. Fuelled by economic growth and protected by unions and government social welfare policies, North Americans left the economic devastation of the pre-war years behind.

Much of the growth in Canada was spurred on by its economic relationship with the U.S., best symbolized by the building of the St. Lawrence Seaway. As economic integration deepened, there was increasing concern that Canada should remain distinct from its neighbour economically, socially, culturally, and politically. The Pipeline Debate in 1956 focused attention on this matter. C.D. Howe argued that the pipeline must run exclusively within Canada. Yet he set up a private syndicate of Canadian and American investors that was seen as a sacrifice of Canadian interests for American financing.

Meanwhile, Canada's military developed closer ties to the U.S. in Cold War conflicts. Our commitment to the principles of the United Nations was shown by our participation in the Korean War alongside American and international troops. Canada and the United States jointly built the Distant Early Warning (DEW) Line of radar stations above the Arctic Circle between 1954 and 1957. In 1958, the two countries combined their missile and air defence forces to form the North American Air Defence Command (NORAD) for continental protection from the Soviet threat. As the decade came to a close, Canadians were shocked after the Canadian-built Avro Arrow, the world's most advanced supersonic jet/interceptor, was cancelled in favour of American Bomarc missiles. This gave rise to speculation that American pressure had led to the plane's demise.

Both countries faced cultural upheaval during the decade. Canada experienced the beginnings of multiculturalism at the same time as the Civil Rights movement was beginning to shake the segregationist foundations of the American South. A new popular culture, embodied in beatnik lifestyles and rock and roll, arose to challenge the conservative mythology of a "Father Knows Best" society. Cultural and entertainment industries began to challenge the norms of traditional life in North America: musicians Elvis Presley, Chuck Berry, and Paul Anka; actors James Dean and Marlon Brando; and artists Jackson Pollock and Harold Town. Teenagers expressed themselves in ways that angered and confounded their parents. The seeds of a "generation gap" were planted.

THE MASSEY COMMISSION

THE ROYAL COMMISSION ON NATIONAL DEVELOPMENT IN THE ARTS, LETTERS AND SCIENCES, 1951

26. American influences on Canadian life to say the least are impressive. There should be no thought of interfering with the liberty of all Canadians to enjoy them. Cultural exchanges are excellent in themselves.… It cannot be denied, however, that a vast and disproportionate amount of material coming from a single alien source may stifle rather than stimulate our own creative effort; and, passively accepted without any standard of comparison, this may weaken critical faculties. We are now spending millions to maintain a national independence which would be nothing but an empty shell without a vigorous and distinctive cultural life.…

▲ This Act, often referred to as the "Massey Commission," was established by Privy Council Order on 8 April 1949, chaired by Vincent Massey *(right)*, who later became the first native-born Governor General of Canada. The Commission was instrumental in the establishment of the National Library and many other groups.

AMERICAN CULTURAL INFLUENCES

◀ In response to Disney's "Davy Crockett" craze, the Canadian series *Radisson/Tomahawk* exploited the legend of a similar French-Canadian frontier hero named "Pierre Esprit Radisson." There were even "Radisson" hats for sale which resembled Davy Crockett's coonskin caps without the tail.

"We dream in French and in English but we work and we entertain ourselves more and more in American."

— Jules Leger, 1957

Canada Council: Massey Commission's Recommendations

(1) The strengthening by money grants and in other ways of certain of the Canadian voluntary organizations on whose active well-being the work of the council will in large measure depend.

(2) The encouragement of Canadian music, drama and ballet (through the appropriate voluntary agencies and co-operation with the CBS and NFB) by such means as the underwriting of tours, the commissioning of music for events of national importance and the establishment of awards to young people of promise whose talents have been revealed in national festivals of music, drama or the ballet.

(3) The promotions of a knowledge of Canada abroad by such means as foreign tours by Canadian lecturers, and by performers in music, ballet and drama and by the exhibition abroad of Canadian art in its varied forms.

▲ A key recommendation of the report led to the creation of the Canada Council in 1957 to foster and promote Canadian arts, humanities, and social sciences.

THE PIPELINE DEBATE

Public Ownership Moves Up As Pipeline Solution

In Parliament yesterday the lines were drawn for a great debate on the transcontinental gas pipeline project. Rt. Hon. C.D. Howe put the best possible face on the government's policy, but in fact revealed nothing new to recommend it. The three chief objections to the present plan remain:

1. The pipeline would be under the domination of American gas and oil interests.
2. Public funds would be used for the benefit of a private corporation.
3. There is no assurance of an early start on the line.

— *Toronto Daily Star,* 16 March 1956

(Callan/The Toronto Star/NAC C 143285)

▸ The Pipeline Debate in 1956 was one of the most contentious in the history of the House of Commons. The opposition parties were concerned about U.S. control of Trans-Canada Pipelines and the CCF even called for public ownership of the company. The bill passed, however, and by late 1958, a 3 700 km pipeline had been built from Saskatchewan to Montreal.

BRANCH PLANTS IN CANADA

There can be important differences between what is in the best interests of the branch plant in Canada…and the interests of the foreign parent company. In such cases the interests of the parent company will usually prevail. The managers of the parent company will… be responsive to the influences and pressures of government officials, labour unions, and public opinion in their own country.

— Walter Gordon, *A Choice for Canada,* 1966

American firms brought with them new methods of production and management, new skills, and new products. They have added to the strength and vitality of our economic life, and through their initiative and daring in a new land they have created thousands of new jobs for Canadians. They have provided new business opportunities and increased incomes for all of us. They have paid their fair share of taxes and with very few exceptions they have been good corporate citizens. The attack on the foreign corporation is based on the assumption that ownership and control of any significant share of our economy is detrimental to Canada. Yet not one bit of concrete evidence has been produced to support the contention that foreign ownership poses a threat to our economic, social or political well-being.

— Stanley Randall, Ontario minister of trade and development (1960s), letter to *Toronto Star,* 23 March 1970

(Courtesy of Dofasco)

▸ In the 1950s, some Canadian companies, such as Dofasco, urged people to buy from Canadian-owned corporations.

BRANCH PLANTS

CANADA
Advantages
• creates jobs
• pays taxes; local, national
• transfer of new technology

Profits

Major Decisions

UNITED STATES
Disadvantages
• profits leave country
• decisions impacting workers made outside country
• most research done outside of country
• can pressure governments to make concessions for them

THE ST. LAWRENCE SEAWAY

...You are no doubt aware that in this area are located industrial plants comprising approximately one-half of Canada's total manufacturing capacity. Many critical materials supplying the defence industries of both Canada and the United States are produced there.... The development of the power potential of the St. Lawrence River is thus a matter of prime importance and urgency to Canada.... Indeed, all the necessary legislation has been enacted, and all other prerequisite steps have been taken to enable the deep waterway to be constructed either by Canada alone or under mutually agreeable arrangements....

— Letter from L.B. Pearson, Minister of External Affairs, to John Foster Dulles, U.S. Secretary of State

The Great Transplanting
New Life for 6,500
— *Toronto Telegram,* 29 June 1959

SEAWAY WON'T WAIT FOR U.S.—ST. LAURENT
Still ready to build seaway alone unless U.S. gets a move on

— *Toronto Star,* 7 May 1954

(NAC PA 93725)

YANKEES! HANDS OFF OUR SEAWAY

The threat of a Canadian-only seaway convinced the U.S. to get involved and work started in 1954. New hydro-electric dams and locks were built; thousands of acres were submerged and entire towns were relocated. The Seaway was officially opened in June 1959.

Thunder Bay, Duluth, Superior, Lake Superior, Sault Ste. Marie, Green Bay, Lake Michigan, Lake Huron, Milwaukee, Goderich, Chicago, Sarnia, Toronto, Burns Harbor, Detroit, Monroe, Toledo, Windsor, Lake Erie, Hamilton, Lake Ontario, Oswego, Buffalo, Conneaut, Lorain, Ashtabula, Cleveland, Oshawa, Prescott, Ogdensburg, Oswego, CANADA, UNITED STATES, Québec, Trois-Rivieres, Montreal, Valleyfield, Becancour, Sorel, Sept-Iles, Port-Cartier, Baie-Comeau, ATLANTIC OCEAN

NORAD

NORAD is a new concept in air defence which welds all the components of defence, regardless of service, into an integrated command that can take to the offensive in a matter of minutes. As an integral part of NORAD, Canada is, perhaps for the first time, participating in a major operational command as an equal partner...

— *Toronto Daily Star,* 20 November 1957

No Need To Telephone Mr. Diefenbaker

Defence Minister Pearkes has now made it clear that the United States general in charge of the North American air defence command can send fighter aircraft out to shoot down enemy bombers without waiting for permission from Ottawa or Washington.

— *Toronto Daily Star,* 6 December 1957

▲ NORAD Cheyenne Mountain complex.

(DND)

Music from NORAD
THE NORAD Commanders
THE NORTH AMERICAN AIR DEFENSE COMMAND
VOLUME I

...An important mission of the band is to depict musically the unanimity of the U.S. and Canadian forces represented in the vast and vital NORAD system...two hundred thousand men and women...on alert 24 hours a day. The protection of this continent from possible enemy air attack is the primary mission of NORAD...

— Back cover, *Music from NORAD,* vol. I

...Canada can contribute more to the defence of democracy, the West, the North American continent and to its own defence as a neutral than as a member of a lop-sided alliance in NORAD... I believe that Canada can speak to the world in the language of freedom and peace to inspire mankind, much as the United States did before the cares of paramountcy, the need to placate dictators, the burden of arming and subsidizing half the world, and the objective and subjective handicaps of wealth...

— James M. Minifie, *Peacemaker or Powder-Monkey,* 1959

1959
20 Feb: PM Diefenbaker cancels
Avro Arrow fighter jet program

1959
26 June: President Eisenhower,
PM Diefenbaker, and Queen Elizabeth II
officially open St. Lawrence Seaway

1959
Canada recognizes Revolutionary
Government of Cuba

JOINT DEFENCE

DISTANT EARLY WARNING SYSTEM, MID-CANADA LINE AND CONTINENTAL AIR DEFENCE 460

3. For the past four years, work has been going on at high priority on the construction of a large and costly radar chain which is required not only to detect enemy bombers but also to control fighter aircraft engaged in the task of interception. This radar chain is known as the Pinetree Chain.

5....The system will extend over 5,000 miles and its survey will involve the examination of a great number of possible sites.... To avoid stationing large numbers of men in this difficult country, the system is being designed to operate with as few men as possible. In overcoming the various technical problems involved the United States Air Force is working closely with the Royal Canadian Air Force...

8. The defence of North America is part of the defence of the North Atlantic region to which both Canada and the United States are pledged as signatories of the North Atlantic Treaty....

— L.B. Pearson, Secretary of State for External Affairs, Public Statement on Continental Defence, 31 March 1954

Missed Bogie

It was the fall of 1961, on a quiet Arctic night. But then most Arctic nights on the DEW Line were quiet. Tom Billowich and I were half way through the midnight to 8:00 am shift at *CAM Four,* Pelly Bay. It was Tom's turn to man the console so I went off to do some preventative maintenance routines (PMs) on the air/ground transmitters in the transmitter room.

It was somewhere around 4:15-4:30 when all hell broke loose. We received a call from FOX Main to do an immediate minimum discernible signal (MDS) test on both beams of the FPS-19 radar system. There was no mistaking the sense of urgency. I called the console and asked Tom what was up. "There's something wrong with the radar," he told me. "We missed a target."

I hotfooted it to the Radar room and did the tests. No problem. The radar was just fine. What was going on? Back to the console room where Tom told me that both CAM Three and Five on each side of us had reported the target but we weren't painting it. I looked at the right-hand screen of the console. We were sure

▲ The radar console where Tom apparently fell asleep and missed seeing the target (bogie) on the right-side screen.

as hell painting it now. What gives?

I asked Tom what was going on. All he would tell me is that we missed the bogie and he was now in deep doodoo. He denied dozing off. I sent him off to do another MDS test for himself and he returned to confirm my earlier results. There was nothing wrong with the system. He really was in trouble....

Before the end of the shift we were informed that Tom should...be ready for pick-up later in the day... They put him directly on the southbound flight, out of the arctic, and out of a job....

— Brian Jeffrey (formerly Brian Simon), 2003

CANCELLATION OF THE AVRO ARROW

A-Arms Defence: Lunacy For Canada

...The issue is whether Canada adopt atomic missiles as an integral step of meshing North American defences into a single whole. Within such a system the United States would be boss. Canada would retain its internal autonomy, but in effect foreign policy would be taken over by the United States.... The cost will be crushing... Everything which helps deter an attack on Canada is in our interests. Anything which makes an attack more probable is not...

— Editorial, *The Star Weekly Magazine,* 12 December 1958

> " No one advocates building buggies in the age of motor cars."
>
> — PM Diefenbaker, 24 February 1959

Diefenbaker Surrenders Our Sovereignty?

History may record that it was John Diefenbaker — staunch Canadian nationalist — who had the unhappy task of yielding a portion of his nation's sovereignty into U.S. hands. This is the ironic judgment that some day may await the prime minister for his historic decision...to kill the Avro Arrow and propel Canada's defence forces into the nuclear age. Never again, it appears, will Canada be able to follow an independent course in seeking its own national security.... Within two or three years, our air defence squadrons may disappear, replaced by U.S. fighter squadrons manned by U.S. pilots on Canadian soil. Our army and navy will be equipped with nuclear weapons but will not be permitted to fire them except with the consent of Washington.

— *Toronto Daily Star,* front page, 23 February 1959

Full marks must be given the Diefenbaker government for facing up to basic military facts. Cancellation of the $400,000,000 Arrow jet interceptor program represents a turning point in Canadian defence policy.... Canada simply cannot afford to defend her own shores by herself.... On the basis of population, Canada's effort should be about one-tenth of the American effort. Canada has neither the industrial capacity, the know-how, nor enough money to assume any massive defence commitment. It is to be hoped that Canadian participation in the Bomarc program — the guided missile ground-to-air defence system which is to replace the Arrow interceptor — will be the start of a Canadian U.S. move toward the integration of weapon production for the defence of North America....

— "Harsh Cold War Realities," *Regina Leader Post,* 24 February 1959

1960 - 1969

1960	1961
19 Oct: Canada and U.S. agree to undertake a joint Columbia River project	15 June: Royal Commission on Publications

THE SIXTIES WAS one of the most turbulent decades experienced in the 20th century. New ideas, new ways of style and dress, new forms of expression, and experimentation developed as young people began to gather in places like Toronto's Yorkville and Vancouver's Gastown, New York's Greenwich Village, and San Francisco's Haight-Ashbury. The youthful idealism of the baby-boom generation found expression in a commitment to the achievement of human and civil rights, especially in the American South; in the anti-Vietnam War movement; and in the American Peace Corps and the Company of Young Canadians. There was a common belief that, with love and understanding, the world could be transformed into a more just place.

An air of optimism was created in both the United States and in Canada with the election of John Fitzgerald Kennedy in November of 1960. Nevertheless, Cold War issues, especially differing attitudes toward Castro's Cuba, unsettled Canadian-American relations. The failed American-sponsored invasion of the Bay of Pigs and the Cuban Missile Crisis intensified the ill-will between Prime Minister Diefenbaker and President Kennedy. As American involvement in the Vietnam War intensified, Canada's policy became more confused. On one hand, our industries supplied materials to the American military; while on the other hand, Canada became a haven for young Americans wanting to evade compulsory military service. Prime Minister Pearson publicly criticized the American bombing of North Vietnam, yet quietly agreed to arm the BOMARC missiles stationed in Canada with nuclear warheads.

During the Sixties, there was an increase in economic and cultural nationalism within Canada. The branch plant economy that had grown throughout the 20th century was being reconfigured by the negotiation of the Auto Pact. Nationalism spread to Canada's labour movement which struggled to wrest control from their American parent organizations. Canada's unions became a strong voice encouraging Canadian control of business, investment, and social institutions, just as Quebec unions were demanding more Québecois control over the key instruments of Quebec's economy and society. Despite this, Canadian business remained dependent on Wall Street investment throughout the 1960s.

Differences in social policy were even greater than economic differences as Canadians strengthened their commitment to both publicly-funded health care and official bilingualism and multiculturalism. As the decade closed, an air of national optimism pervaded Canada with the success of Expo '67 and the election of a strong, self-assured and cosmopolitan Prime Minister, Pierre Trudeau.

CUBAN MISSILE CRISIS

▸ Cuban Missile Crisis Map. The relationship between President Kennedy and PM Diefenbaker, already strained, was further worsened during the Cuban Missile Crisis when Kennedy made no attempt to consult Diefenbaker at any time.

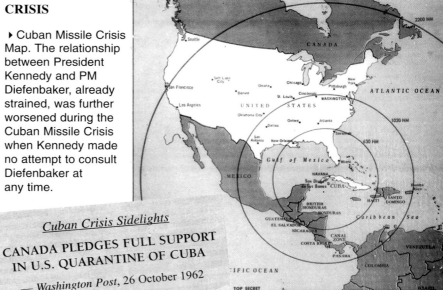

Cuban Crisis Sidelights

CANADA PLEDGES FULL SUPPORT IN U.S. QUARANTINE OF CUBA

— *Washington Post*, 26 October 1962

"…Within the past week unmistakable evidence has established the fact that a series of offensive missile sites is now in preparation on that imprisoned island. The purpose of these bases can be none other than to provide a nuclear strike capability against the Western Hemisphere…It shall be the policy of this nation to regard any nuclear missile launched from Cuba against any nation in the Western Hemisphere as an attack by the Soviet Union on the United States, requiring a full retaliatory response upon the Soviet Union.…"

— President John F. Kennedy, Television Address, 22 October 1962

"…I considered that [Kennedy] was perfectly capable of taking the world to the brink of thermonuclear destruction to prove himself the man for our times, a courageous champion of Western democracy…Canada certainly had the right to expect notice longer than two hours, if military measures were to be involved. NORAD had worked out…secret procedures for consultation to be invoked when a threat to North American security was perceived. It was obvious that Canada was not to be consulted but was expected to accept without question the course to be determined by the President. The partnership in continental defence that my government had worked out with the Eisenhower administration could not long survive the strains imposed upon it by President Kennedy."

— Excerpt from Prime Minister John Diefenbaker's Memoirs *Diefenbaker, John. One Canada, Vol.3: The Tumultuous Years, 1962 to 1967*

"This is a time for calmness…. The determination of Canadians will be that the United Nations should be charged at the earliest possible moment with this serious problem…. I suggest that…perhaps the eight nations comprising the unaligned members of the 18 nation disarmament committee, be given the opportunity of making an on-site inspection in Cuba to ascertain what the facts are, a major step forward would be taken.…"

— Diefenbaker in reaction to the crisis, House of Commons debates, 22 October 1962

"We worry when you look hard at us, but we are touchy about being overlooked."

— Lester B. Pearson at an address at Notre Dame University, quoted in *New York Times*, 1963

COLUMBIA RIVER TREATY

Treaty relating to cooperative development of the water resources of the Columbia River Basin Done 17 January 1961

<u>Development by the United States of America Respecting Power</u>

(1) The United States of America shall maintain and operate the hydro-electric facilities included in the base system and any additional hydro-electric facilities constructed on the main arm of the Columbia River in the United States of America in a manner that makes the most effective use of the improvement in stream flow resulting from operation of the Canadian storage for hydroelectric power generation in the United States of America power system.

The Columbia River Treaty went into effect in 1964. The treaty provided for building four storage reservoirs: three in Canada and one in the U.S. These dams added much needed flood control and allowed for more efficient use of the hydro-electric resources.

THE NUCLEAR DEBATE

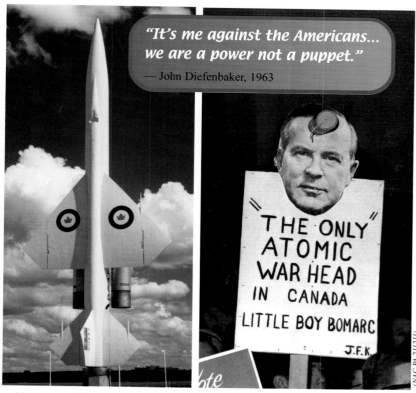

"It's me against the Americans... we are a power not a puppet."
— John Diefenbaker, 1963

"THE ONLY" ATOMIC WAR HEAD IN CANADA LITTLE BOY BOMARC J.F.K.

(NAC PA 211211)

▲ Under the NORAD agreement signed between Canada and the U.S., 56 Bomarc anti-aircraft missiles were set up in Canada. However, overwhelming protests against the installation of nuclear warheads on the Bomarcs kept it from happening until 1963 under Pearson's government.

"...there are some who say to me that if you take a stand like this [on the Bomarc missiles] it is anti-American...it is nothing of the kind. I do not think it is other than pro-Canadian, or Canadian, to point out when something is wrong... I believe in cooperation because I believe in good relations... But I cannot accept the fears of those who believe we must be subservient in order to be a good ally of any country in the world..."

— John Diefenbaker, House of Commons, 5 February 1963

...The key issue is atomic weapons. If we need them, we should take steps to get them from the United States on the best terms that can be arranged. But no argument has been made out that we do need them, while an impressive argument can be made that we are better off, defensively, without them. And if this is so, then the great bulk of our expenditures on aircraft, missiles, ships and so on is a waste of money because we cannot afford enough of them to be of any real use, when conventionally armed, against the threat facing us.

— "Nuclear Madness," *Toronto Daily Star*, 17 November 1958

New Pearson Nuclear Plan Stirs Up Mixed Reaction

Liberal Leader Lester Pearson's decision to commit his party to accepting nuclear weapons for Canada's armed forces has brought powerful pressure on Prime Minister Diefenbaker to clarify the government's position. Mr. Pearson, in a Toronto speech...said a future Liberal government would accept the weapons for Canadian forces..."only until it could renegotiate a new defence policy."...

— *Toronto Daily Star*, 14 January 1963

Befuddlement Over Bomarcs

Canada's gamble with the Bomarc B is rapidly becoming a "heads we lose, tails we lose," proposition. This ground-to-air missile we are procuring from the Americans has never been test-fired successfully, and failed for the sixth time Saturday at Cape Canaveral, Fla. Yet Defence Minister Pearkes is undismayed, and will press on with construction of the two Bomarc installations in Canada which will cost Canadian taxpayers $125 million....

— *Toronto Daily Star*, 25 March 1960

"If we scratch Bomarc, we have stuck the Canadians for a whole mess of them and we have another problem on our border."

— Daniel J. Flood, U.S. House of Representatives, 6 February 1963

1960 — 1969

THE AUTOPACT

▸ The Auto Pact, signed in January 1965, was meant to reduce taxes on vehicles and parts in both countries, and created a single North American market.

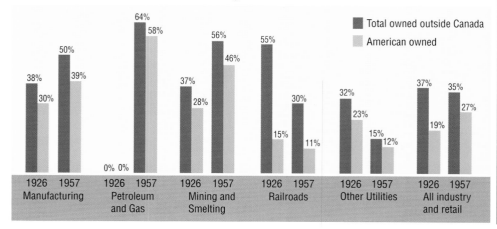

Legend:
- Total owned outside Canada
- American owned

	1926	1957
Manufacturing	38% / 30%	50% / 39%
Petroleum and Gas	0% / 0%	64% / 58%
Mining and Smelting	37% / 28%	56% / 46%
Railroads	55% / 15%	30% / 11%
Other Utilities	32% / 23%	15% / 12%
All industry and retail	37% / 19%	35% / 27%

Canada-United States Automotive Products Agreement of 1965 ("Auto Pact")

Under the terms of the Auto Pact, qualified motor vehicle manufacturers are able to import both vehicles and original equipment automotive parts duty-free from any Most Favoured Nation country, provided the following performance requirements are met:

(a) The value of vehicles produced in Canada must meet or exceed a specified proportion of the manufacturer's annual sales in Canada. In other words, if manufacturers want to sell imported cars duty-free in Canada they must also build cars in Canada....

VIETNAM

CANADA AND THE UNITED STATES – PRINCIPLES FOR PARTNERSHIP –

Article 55: In consultation with the United States, Canadian authorities must have confidence that the practice of quiet diplomacy is not only neighbourly and convenient to the United States but that it is in fact more effective than the alternative of raising a row.... By the same token, the United States authorities must be satisfied that, in such consultations, Canada will have sympathetic regard for the worldwide preoccupation and responsibilities of the United States....

▴ Joint Report by A.D.P. Heeney (Canada) and Livingston Merchant (U.S.), 28 June 1965. "Quiet diplomacy" was fostered by a strong political lobby during the 1960s when the U.S. was "preoccupied" with the Vietnam War. However, Canadians who opposed the war advocated an "independent" approach in relations.

◂ Protesters march not only against the war in Vietnam but also against Canadian arms sales to the United States for use in that war.

(Provincial Archives of Alberta)

"...*Blood money to the tune of more than $300 million a year.*"
— Tommy Douglas, NDP leader

"If it were a question of morality and if I felt that it were bad to sell arms to the United States in a moral sense then I would have to feel that it's bad also to sell them nickel and asbestos and airplane components."

— Former PM Pierre Trudeau, 1968, to CBC interviewer Patrick Watson

"... There are many factors which I am not in a position to weigh, but there does appear to be at least a possibility that a suspension of such air strikes against North Vietnam, at the right time, might provide the Hanoi authorities with the opportunity, if they wish to take it, to inject some flexibility into their policy without appearing to do so as a direct result of military pressure..."

— Pearson, speech at Temple University, 2 April 1965

"Give Lester my best...and tell him that if he has any more speeches to make on Viet Nam to please make them outside of the United States."

— President Johnson, 1965, cited in J.L. Granatstein, *For Better or For Worse*, 1991

▴ Prime Minister Pearson's speech at Temple University, an appeal to avoid escalating the Vietnam conflict, was given on American soil and infuriated President Lyndon Johnson.

CULTURE

> *Canadians are generally indistinguishable from the Americans, and the surest way of telling the two apart is to make the observation to a Canadian.*
>
> — Richard Starnes, U.S. journalist, cited in *Canada: The Uneasy Neighbour*, by Gerald Clark, 1965

BROADCASTING ACT – 7 March 1968

2.(b) The Canadian broadcasting system should be effectively owned and controlled by Canadians so as to safeguard, enrich and strengthen the cultural, political, social and economic fabric of Canada….

(d) The programming provided by the Canadian broadcasting system should be varied and comprehensive and should provide reasonable, balanced opportunity for the expression of differing views on matters of public concern, and the programming provided by each broadcaster should be of high standards, using predominantly Canadian creative and other resources…

5.(1) There shall be a commission to be known as the Canadian Radio-Television Commission consisting of five full-time members and ten part-time members to be appointed by the Governor in Council…

▲ The "hippie" and peace movement greatly influenced Canadian culture and music in the sixties.

▶ Canada's *The Guess Who* released "American Woman," a musical metaphor for concerns about American cultural influence, in 1970. When the band played the White House that same year, First Lady Pat Nixon asked that the song be dropped from the set.

> *American Woman, said get away…*
> *I don't need your war machines*
> *I don't need your ghetto scenes…*

The border between the United States and Canada is the most friendly and least visible line of international power in the world. It is crossed daily by thousands of travellers who hardly notice it in their passage. It is washed by a Niagara of genial oratory and illuminated, or sometimes obscured, by a perpetual diplomatic dialogue. On both sides the border is taken as a fact of nature, almost as an act of God, which no man thinks of changing.

— Bruce Hutchinson, Canadian writer and editor, 1966

Let me say it should not be surprising if of our policies in many instances either reflect or take into account the proximity of the United States. Living next to you is in some ways like sleeping with an elephant: no matter how friendly and even tempered the beast one is affected by every twitch and grunt…

— Pierre Trudeau, National Press Club Washington, D.C., 25 March 1969

ARCTIC SOVEREIGNTY

▶ The Arctic became vital for North American defence against the Soviet Union. The Canadian government saw support for the Inuit as a way of claiming sovereignty over the Arctic and gave millions of dollars, often repositioning their settlements to advance Canada's claim.

▲ *CCGS John A. MacDonald* escorting the tanker Manhattan through the Northwest Passage to Prudhoe Bay, Alaska, August 1969. The navigation of the Northwest Passage by the SS Manhattan in September, 1969 raised concerns over Canadian sovereignty in the Arctic. The Trudeau government enacted the Arctic Waters Pollution Act in 1970 in an attempt to control shipping in the passage but it was not until 1988 that a Canada-U.S. agreement was reached. American icebreakers were allowed to cross Arctic waters but only with case-by-case approval.

ANTHONY JENKINS/The Globe and Mail.

1970-1979

1970	1970
May: CRTC introduces 60% Canadian content regulations for radio and television	October Crisis

FOR CANADIANS, the preservation of an independent economy and culture was the major focus in the 1970s. A late 1960s "Buy Canadian" program had blossomed into a political movement fuelled by economic nationalism. Canadian content regulations for radio, television, and magazines helped protect and promote Canadian artists, writers and musicians. The CRTC, the CBC, and the Foreign Investment Review Agency were expressions of a determination to remain independent from our neighbour to the South.

The Guess Who achieved chart-topping North American success with their cautionary metaphor, "American Woman." Prime Minster Trudeau set a lighter tone when he quipped before the National Press Club in Washington, "Living next to you is like sleeping with an elephant." Tensions between the two countries, and especially between Trudeau and President Richard Nixon, grew throughout the early part of the decade, as Canada asserted an independent foreign policy. Divisions were expressed over such issues as our opposition to the Vietnam War and acceptance of American draft dodgers, the recognition of Communist China, and our continuing relationship with Fidel Castro's Cuba. In spite of these political tensions, Canadians continued to share an unprotected border, responsibilities in NORAD, and a joint interest in a strong North American economy.

The October Crisis of 1970 was a matter of grave concern for Canadians. White House observers and the Pentagon worried that the crisis in Quebec could destabilize its largest trading partner and most important military ally. The Americans considered the possibility of military intervention if the crisis in Quebec threatened Canadian Confederation. Reports of American troop movements amassing in Oswego, New York circulated in Canada.

Trade and foreign policy continued to create tension between the two countries. Despite the fact that the United States had been moving towards formal recognition of Communist China since 1971, President Gerald Ford expressed opposition to China's participation in the 1976 Montreal summer Olympic games. When Jimmy Carter became President, Trudeau had a confidante in Washington who shared a similar global outlook. To heal divisions created by the Vietnam War, President Carter granted amnesty to Americans who had evaded the draft, reversing the American exodus to Canada. Similar views on major environmental issues also led to closer cooperation between the American EPA and Canadian environmental agencies.

Relations between the two countries were never better than when Ken Taylor, Canada's ambassador to Iran, and his staff, rescued six US Embassy officials during the Tehran hostage incident in November 1979. Canadian-American relations were back on track.

THE AMERICAN INFLUENCE ON MEDIA

MR. BEDARD: [W]hen one is flooded by American magazines, when one is deluged by sensational magazines, when we watch our children go up to a newsstand to purchase Playboy and similar magazines, when we attempt to offer them educational magazines (magazines which will make them respectable citizens) — what do we get? We get rubbish....

MR FORTIER: What worried me a little is the control you suggest over the free flow of information on the pretext that a given magazine is not as good as yours....

MR. BEDARD: Mr. Fortier, it is impossible for us to inundate our American friends however, you will agree that they can destroy us. Given this fact, we can be realistic enough to say that we want to be friends, that we are desirous of free exchange. However, when it is a question of culture, of the education of our population however, we wish to retain a certain control; we are not Americans, we are Canadians.

— Testimony of Simon Bedard, Vice-President of *Actualité* magazine, before the Senate of Canada, Proceedings of the Special Committee on Mass Media, 19 February 1970

BECOME MORE CANADIAN WHILE YOU SLEEP THROUGH CBC RADIO AND TELEVISION!

ASTONISHING BUT TRUE!

HOW TO CANADIANIZE YOUR MIND AND BODY WHILE YOU SLEEP THROUGH CBC RADIO AND TELEVISION!

Deep Sleep Canadianization in Painless Lessons
$3.00
By Harry Boil

NOW YOU CAN:

- Develop a stronger Canadian consciousness
- Erase your unhealthy addiction to "Sixty Minutes" and "Kojak"
- Learn to watch National Film Board shorts without grimacing
- Control your desire to turn the channel while watching "Man Alive"
- Discover the secret of why Barbara Frum laughs at Larry Zolf and Patrick McFadden on "As It Happens"
- Learn to make real Canadian candy-floss in your bathtub, listening to "This Country In The Morning"

THE CANADIANIZED BROADCASTING CORPORATION
A Division of Bureaucrat Enterprises

▲ This imaginary ad appeared in a paperback book prepared by people associated with the humorous CBC radio program "Inside from the Outside."

Finally, in the area of broadcasting I really want to support the proposal of the CRTC which as you know is that programming should be 60 percent Canadian content on television and even more important that the prime time or prime hours when most people are viewing, I think 50 percent of that has to be — two hours out of four have to be Canadian and that on radio 30 percent of the music played has to be Canadian in some way, even if it is only Lorne Greene, who holds Canadian citizenship recording a new record on the set of Bonanza.... I think the thing that has been wrong in broadcasting in this country is that the philosophy we have had has been an American philosophy — not a Canadian philosophy — a philosophy that sees that broadcasting is an arm of the marketplace.... We have to sing our own songs and we have to create our own heroes, dream our own dreams or we won't have a country at all.

— Testimony of Pierre Berton before the Senate of Canada Proceedings of the Special Committee on Mass Media, 25 March 1970

"We don't need to defend ourselves against the world, but to express ourselves to the world." — Joe Clark, 1978

THE WAR IN VIETNAM

MANUAL FOR DRAFT-AGE IMMIGRANTS TO CANADA

Slowly at first, and now in growing numbers…young Americans are coming to Canada to resist the draft. There is no draft in Canada…. Immigration is not the best choice for everyone and this pamphlet does not take sides. Four other alternatives are open to draft-age Americans: deferment, C.O. [conscientious objector] status, jail or the armed forces… Canada is not an easy way out; in many cases it means cutting yourself off from parents and friends. But there are many reasons draft resisters have chosen Canada — as many reasons as Americans.

(CP Photo)

▶ Demonstrators at the Suffield Coalition rally in Medicine Hat 3 July 1972, protesting British training and Canadian research projects at Canadian Forces Base Suffield.

"This Canadian thinks it is time to speak up for the Americans as the most generous and possibly the least appreciated people on earth…. Our neighbours have faced it alone, and I'm one Canadian who is damned tired of hearing them get kicked around. They will come out of this thing with their flag held high. And when they do, they are entitled to thumb their nose at the lands that are gloating over their present troubles. I hope Canada is not one of those."

— Gordon Sinclair, "The Americans," Original Script, "LET'S BE PERSONAL" Broadcast 5 June 1973, CFRB, Toronto

Vietnam Era Coming to End for War Resisters in Canada

The war resisters here are ageing now, blending more and more into Canadian life, moving into their thirties and many of them have long since become Canadian citizens. They are remembered as their punchy and determined magazine *Amex-Canada,* meaning American exiles in Canada, is published for the last time with an eighty-page issue…The current editor, who deserted in 1968 as a ROTC, soon goes home after almost a decade in Canadian exile. He is one of thousands of war resisters here, in the United States and abroad, who were pardoned under president Carter's second amnesty offer which expired last October 4. According to *Amex-Canada,* about sixty percent of the estimated 20,000 war resisters who fled to Canada since 1968 will not be going home…..

— *Miami Herald,* 22 November 1977

"Clearly, there was no way the United States should have been there in the first place."…

— Pierre Trudeau, *Memoirs,* 1993

TRUDEAU-NIXON RELATIONS

(CP PHOTO file)

"A complex man, full of self-doubts… very strange."

— Trudeau on Nixon, B.W. Powe, *The Solitary Outlaw,* 1987

FBI Spied on Canada's Pierre Trudeau for 30 Years

Newly obtained records show the FBI kept secret files about Pierre Trudeau for three decades, from his early days as an intellectual rabble-rouser in the 1950s through his tenure as prime minister. The files, released to the *Citizen,* reveal the Federal Bureau of Investigation maintained an active interest in Mr. Trudeau, even passing clandestinely gathered information about his 1973 trip to China to Nixon administration officials…. On three occasions in 1973, the FBI relayed information concerning Mr. Trudeau to officials in the administration of then-president Richard Nixon, including Secretary of State Henry Kissinger….

— Jim Bronskill, *The Ottawa Citizen,* 20 January 2001

"In our dealings, I can't say there was any warmth of feeling on either side."

— Pierre Trudeau, *Memoirs,* 1993

1970 – 1979

GREAT LAKES WATER QUALITY AGREEMENT

Great Lakes Water Quality Agreement of 1972
Preamble

The Government of the United States of America and the Government of Canada; Determined to restore and enhance water quality in the Great Lakes System; Seriously concerned about the grave deterioration of water quality on each side of the boundary to an extent that is causing injury to health and property on the other side, as described in the 1970 report of the International Joint Commission on Pollution of Lake Erie, Lake Ontario and the International Section of the St. Lawrence River; Intent upon preventing further pollution of the Great Lakes System...Reaffirming...the rights and obligations of both countries under the Boundary Waters Treaty...and in particular their obligation not to pollute boundary waters; Recognizing the rights of each country in the use of its Great Lakes waters; Satisfied that the 1970 report of the International Joint Commission provides a sound basis for new and more effective cooperative actions to restore and enhance water quality in the Great Lakes System; Convinced that the best means to achieve improved water quality in the Great Lakes System is through the adoption of common objectives, the development and implementation of cooperative programs and other measures, and the assignment of special responsibilities and functions to the International Joint Commission; Have agreed as follows:...

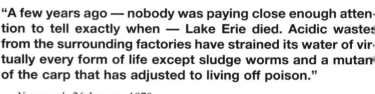

First signed in 1972 and renewed in 1978, the agreement expresses the commitment of each country to restore and maintain the chemical, physical and biological integrity of the Great Lakes Basin Ecosystem and includes a number of objectives and guidelines.

"A few years ago — nobody was paying close enough attention to tell exactly when — Lake Erie died. Acidic wastes from the surrounding factories have strained its water of virtually every form of life except sludge worms and a mutant of the carp that has adjusted to living off poison."

— *Newsweek,* 26 January 1970

1978 Water Quality Agreement
Signed by U.S. and Canada

A new agreement was signed today between Canada and the United States calling for programs and measures to further abate pollution in the Great Lakes.... Environmental Protection Agency Deputy Administrator Barbara Blum, a co-signer of the agreement, praised the cooperative efforts of the International Joint Commission in bringing about this new agreement. "This cooperative effort reaffirms our determination to restore and enhance the quality of Great Lakes water...The initial agreement in 1972 resulted in considerable progress, and this new agreement will go even further in supporting the drinking water needs of more than 35 million people."

The 1978 Great Lakes Water Quality Agreement builds on six years of experience under the Great Lakes Water Quality Agreement of 1972. Since it came into effect, there has been a significant improvement in understanding of the technical and scientific aspect of water quality, the presence and effects of toxic substances in the Great Lakes System and the extent of non-point source pollution....[T]he specific objectives of the 1978 Agreement are far more comprehensive and stringent than those of the 1972 Agreement.

— EPA press release, 22 November 1978

CONTINENTAL DRIFT

"What is Canadian culture?... Well it's like a melting pot here...you get all kinds... [D]o Canadians wear funny suits? Do they smell odd? Is it something in the water? I've been here for about ten weeks now and the only difference that I've found is that when you pick up a jar that says 'Peanut Butter' the other side says, 'Beurre d'arachides.' By sight I can't tell a guy from Moose Jaw from an Indianapolite or whatever they call themselves. Everybody around here seems to speak the same language I do, and I can read the newspaper with no trouble whatsoever... we too, can pick up the phone and call China. It's just that we don't have anything to say.

Maybe culture is what they keep in a box in the Royal Ontario Museum (which is better than anything that I've seen back home by-the-way).

What it comes down to, ladies and gents, is that culture isn't something that can be weighed or thumped or pushed around. It's what you are inside. It's who you really are as you.

And Mr. Nixon can't give it to you. And he can't take it away.

— Henry Morgan, American writer and broadcaster, *Toronto Star,* 10 December 1971

The Canada-U.S. border line drawn on the floor of a pool hall as it passes through a farmhouse on the Vermont/Québec border.

1976
Summer Olympics held
in Montreal

1976
Summit of leading industrial nations
held in San Juan, Puerto Rico

1977
U.S. and Canada extend territorial
waters out to 200 miles to stop
foreign fishing boats

AMERICAN INVESTMENT IN CANADA

THE OPTIONS / 1972
- Canada can seek to maintain more or less its present relationship with the United States with a minimum of policy adjustments;
- Canada can move deliberately toward closer integration with the United States;
- Canada can pursue a comprehensive long-term strategy to develop and strengthen the Canadian economy and other aspects of its national life and in the process to reduce the present Canadian vulnerability.

— Mitchell Sharp, Secretary of State for External Affairs, excerpts from article "Canada-U.S. Relations: Options for the Future," 17 October 1972

"I do think that if you are going to have relative satisfaction of the Canadian people in the long run you are going to have to move gradually to a greater degree of Canadian ownership… there is a great upward surge of nationalism all over the world and it is not just in Canada. You move to a stage where people are resentful. They think they are not getting a fair return out of the assets of their country and I think that feeling has gradually been developing in Canada."

— Edgar Bentsen, former Minister of Finance, on American investment in Canada, *Globe and Mail,* 31 December 1972

▸ The mandate of the Foreign Investment Review Agency, established by the Trudeau Government in 1973, was to examine all applications for acquisitions of Canadian companies and to recommend approval or disapproval. Although the majority of acquisitions were approved, FIRA was strongly opposed by investors.

"You can disagree without being disagreeable."
— U.S. President Gerald Ford, Washington, DC, 1974

The automobile industry today hailed the agreement between the United States and Canada to end tariffs on cars and car parts as a step toward a better economic future for both nations….

— *Port Huron Times Herald*, 16 January 1975

FOREIGN INVESTMENT REVIEW ACT
Assented to 12 December 1973

2. (1) This Act is enacted by the Parliament of Canada in recognition by Parliament that the extent to which control of Canadian industry, trade and commerce has become acquired by persons other than Canadians and the effect thereof on the ability of Canadians to maintain effective control over their economic environment is a matter of national concern….

AUTO TRADE (SELECTED YEARS) Canada-U.S. Trade in Automotive Products (in Canadian $ millions)		
YEAR	Total Export Value to U.S.	Total Import Value from U.S.
1965	$ 250 million	$ 961 million
1967	$ 1520	$ 2042
1969	$ 3309	$ 3399
1971	$ 4040	$ 3842
1973	$ 5299	$ 5727
1975	$ 5903	$ 7822
1977	$ 9861	$10948

(Statistics Canada, Inquiry into the Automobile Industry, October 1979)

AHA! THOUGHT I WAS SLEEPING— EH MOUSE?

JOBS

(Roschov, 1979)

"The Paradox of the Branch Plant"

…Its name is that of a Scottish town. It was built on Lake Simcoe, named for the first British governor of Upper Canada. Many of its first settlers were United Empire Loyalists, Americans loyal to the crown who fled into the harsh countryside of Upper Canada rather than accept republicanism…. The hard economic fact of Barrie's recent history is that it could not afford to perpetuate such ancient concepts of WASP superiority without the postwar inroads of American capital and establishment of new U.S. branch plants.

In late 1945, when World War II ended, Barrie looked like a dying town. It was trying to survive on a depleting Canadian army base, seasonal tourism, railway services and a family-run tannery.

Then, in 1946, General Electric built a plant for manufacturing fractional horsepower motors. Since then, a stream of American firms have built plants here and prospered, Barrie along with them…. Willard Kinzie, ex-mayor, a self-made businessman and one of Barrie's most distinguished citizens, even reversed the trend somewhat when he sold his dairy business to Beatrice Foods company of Chicago, a $2 billion American dairy products multi-national company…. Most citizens in small-town English Canada have the best of two worlds, a proud English-dominated history in which they can indulge nostalgically, an affluent American-dominated present in which they live. It's a paradox of late twentieth-century Canadian nationalism.

— *The Barrie Examiner,* 27 March 1975

AS THE 1980S BEGAN, Canadians were focused on important internal issues. The first referendum on the question of sovereignty association was held in May, 1980. What would be the response if Quebecers voted to remove themselves from Confederation? Would there be a peaceful fracturing of the country, or would Canada use force to keep a reluctant province within its borders? On the surface, this appeared to be a domestic issue. Much to our dismay, there was an anxious spectator who considered its security at risk should there be a new, unfamiliar country created on its borders. The United States considered its military options in the event that a new sovereign Quebec posed a security risk. Its troops gathered at Oswego, New York, as the outcome of the referendum was being determined by Quebecers.

Once the "non" side had won the referendum, Canadian-American relations returned to familiar issues. On security matters, Trudeau was faced with the question of whether to continue the continental security arrangements of his predecessors. In 1981, the Trudeau government signed an agreement to extend the NORAD connection for another five years. Whether this decision also meant becoming a part of President Reagan's "Star Wars" scheme worried many Canadians. In 1983, Trudeau signed another security arrangement with the Americans to allow American cruise missiles to be tested in the Canadian North. The agreement included seed money for an American branch plant of Litton Industries in Toronto to develop a navigational guidance system for the weapon. The value of technological cooperation had already been proven when the first "Canadarm" was used on the maiden voyage of U.S. Space Shuttle Columbia in 1981. Two years later, Canada opened its Canadian Astronaut Program in close collaboration with NASA. Marc Garneau became this country's first astronaut to reach space in 1984 aboard the Space Shuttle Challenger.

The cool relations that had defined most of the Trudeau years were transformed, as if overnight, with the election of Prime Minister Mulroney in 1984. By dismantling such Trudeau initiatives as the Foreign Investment Review Agency and the National Energy Program, the new Prime Minister clearly indicated that Canada was now "open for business" and that our new government would be more in alignment with the United States on issues such as business, investment, economic integration, foreign policy, and culture. Controversial initiatives such as the 1988 Canada-US Free Trade Agreement (FTA) were indicative of this new mindset in Ottawa.

Thus a decade that began with concern about the distinctiveness and sovereignty of Quebec ended with concern and debate about whether closer economic ties with the United States would mean a loss of Canada's distinctiveness and sovereignty.

THE NATIONAL ENERGY PROGRAM (NEP)

Economic Nationalism and Pride in Canada

Canada's major cities and many of its ten provinces are experiencing the largest flow of American tourists in history... The reason for this peaceful Yankee invasion is Canada's shaky dollar... One reason for this decline [to 79 cents] is the loss of confidence by the powerful New York money markets in Canada's slow-moving economy and the resultant decline in American portfolio investments in Canada.... Canada's nationalistic economic policies are culminating in a tough national energy program that will compel the largely American-owned Canadian oil industry to become, by law, fifty percent Canadian-owned no later than 1990.

The nasty rumour gaining credence in Canada is that Prime Minister...Trudeau is promoting it to bind the country together because President Reagan's White House aides, with strong "America first" views, are preparing to take a hard line on the many unresolved economic issues now dividing the two neighbours.

— *The New York Times*, 29 August 1981

▸ Protesting the National Energy Policy. In response to the 1970s oil crisis, the Trudeau government responded with the NEP. By 1979 70% of Canadian oil and gas sales were foreign owned. The NEP was designed to address the issue of foreign ownership of Canada's energy resources. Other economic nationalist programs had been introduced earlier.

THE CANADIAN CAPER

"...[T]he 444 days of the hostage crisis were trying times for this country... We're today honoring [an]...act of courage... Four days after the storming of the American Embassy, Ambassador Taylor received a call from five Americans who had escaped from the Embassy when it was overrun.... Ambassador Taylor immediately recommended to his government in Ottawa that Americans be given shelter. Without any hesitation, the Canadian Government granted the permission. Two days later, the Americans were taken to Ambassador Taylor's residence and that of another Canadian Embassy family, the John Sheardowns. Two weeks later, another American joined his five compatriots. For 79 days, they lived there pretending to be visitors....

...At this point, the Canadian Government in Ottawa and the Embassy began the ingenious preparations for an escape. The Canadian Government agreed to issue fictitious passports to the Americans. The Canadian Embassy staff began making flights in and out of Tehran to establish a travel pattern and to learn airport procedures.

...The medal is inscribed... Entre amis, appreciation for the noble and heroic effort in the harboring of six United States diplomats and safe return to America. Thank you, Canada."

— President Reagan's Presentation of Congressional Gold Medal to Ken Taylor, 16 June 1981

(CP PHOTO/Robert Cooper)

Ambassador Kenneth Taylor gives details as to how the six Americans were smuggled out of Iran, Ottawa, 1980.

LITTON INDUSTRIES BOMBING

▲ Police drag protesters away after the bombing.

We were not trying to threaten or kill the workers or executives of Litton Systems. We were attempting to destroy part of an industrial facility that produces machinery for mass murder. We wanted to blow up as much of that technology of death as possible....

— Communiqué from Direct Action, 17 October 1982

"If we did a bombing, it would make the Americans think twice about giving their Canadian plant the contract to build the guidance system," I said.

"Yeah," Brent added, "and it would show people in the anti-nuclear movement that militant actions can affect political decisions. The Americans don't want to waste money, and they won't like the publicity that blowing up their plant will draw."

— Ann Hansen, cited in *Direct Action: Memoirs of an Urban Guerrilla,* 17 October 1982

CRUISE MISSILE CRISIS

During the Cold War Trudeau angered Reagan by campaigning in an attempt to diffuse tension between the U.S. and the U.S.S.R. In the face of massive domestic opposition and foreign pressure, the Trudeau government allows the U.S. to conduct cruise missile tests in northern Alberta.

"Isn't this something, Harry, the great outdoors... it's so quiet, you could hear a..."

(Tom Innes, Calgary Herald)

Canada has pledged not to develop nuclear weapons, but the Canadian Air Force is still equipped with US-made nuclear missiles... Canada is helping the US with the production and testing of the Cruise missile... And there is steadily mounting outrage at Prime Minister Trudeau's decision to allow the US Air Force to test the Cruise missile system at the Canadian Forces Base in Cold Lake, Alberta, where the rough terrain and climate approximate to conditions in the northern regions of the Soviet Union.

— "Refusing to Cruise," *New Internationalist,* March 1983

"...Our whole negotiation in relationship with NORAD, and the main reason that we [Canada] were involved in NORAD in the defence of North America was to contribute to the defence...of the strategic deterrent that rested in the United States.... The Cruise missile was part of that deterrent force.... It made a whole lot of sense then for us to contribute to the credibility of that deterrent by contribution to the testing of the missile.... Now why should it be important for us to have the missile tested in Canada? Because, by and large, the terrain over which that Cruise missile would have been flying in war, in an attack on the Soviet Union, was very similar to the northern part of Canada, to the Northwest Territories...."

— Donald MacNamara, military officer attached to the Privy Council Office, 1883, cited in *The Big Chill: Canada and the Cold War,* 1998

GENEVA SUMMIT (STRATEGIC DEFENCE INITIATIVE)

We have no intention of pressing any of our allies to participate in this program. It will be entirely up to Canada to decide the extent to which, if at all, it wishes to share in the research efforts. Should Canada decide such participation is in its interests, we would be delighted to work with you in this important undertaking. But let's get this straight about the Strategic Defense Initiative. For more than a generation we have believed no war will begin as long as each side knows the other can retaliate with devastating results. Well, I believe there could be a better way to keep the peace. The Strategic Defense Initiative is a research effort aimed at finding a non-nuclear defense against ballistic missiles...

— U.S. President Ronald Reagan in an interview with *Maclean's,* 18 March 1985

▸ The United States and the USSR begin new arms control negotiations in Geneva, encompassing defence and space systems, strategic nuclear forces, and intermediate-range nuclear forces. They are between an American-Soviet coalition of arms-controllers and an American-Soviet coalition of arms-builders.

We can't control what happens in Geneva this week but defence analysts say the Canadian government should look for ways to reduce the threat of war

(Locher, Chicago Tribune)

1980 — 1989

STRENGTHENING TIES WITH THE U.S.

...I would like to stress at the outset that as prime minister of Canada, I place the highest priority on retaining good relations between Canada and the United States.... Because of your enormous size and influence, the government of Canada must always be vigilant to ensure the protection of our integrity and interests.... Today the most noteworthy measure of our relationship is in our economic ties — in investment, in trade, in technology flows...

Canada is the largest trading partner of the United States.... And your second largest trading partner is not Germany or Japan but Ontario, a province of Canada.

The restoration of good and sound relationships between our two countries is clearly a top priority... We seek trading arrangements which provide fair but also secure access to the U.S. market, unfettered by initiatives aimed at problems caused by other countries but inadvertently hurting Canadian companies....

— Brian Mulroney, notes for speech to The Economic Club of New York, 10 December 1984

> **"Canada is open for business."**
> — Brian Mulroney, 1984

▲ Prime Minister Brian Mulroney answers questions from students regarding free trade at Napanee District Secondary School.

UNITED STATES OF AMERICA CONGRESSIONAL RECORD
CANADIAN RELATIVES

Mr. HATCH: Mr. President, it is of vital importance that we continue to have close, friendly relations with the people and government of our northern neighbour, Canada. In so many areas our interests overlap, and we can truly say our fates are inextricably linked. On national security issues, business and economic issues, environmental issues, natural resource issues, water rights issues, and more, we must continue to work together in a spirit of dialog and compromise to insure that Americans and Canadians are able to carry on our partnership well into the future....

— Washington, 22 April 1986

SHAMROCK SUMMIT

> **"It was a shamrock shuffle with President Reagan calling the tune and Prime Minister Mulroney eagerly dancing along."**
> — Ed Broadbent, NDP leader, 1984

Your trip should open a new chapter in Canadian-American relations, building on your excellent personal relationship with the prime minister. Mulroney has increasingly taken a pro-U.S. stance in foreign affairs and has been more forthcoming on many bilateral issues. The result has been the establishment of a greater degree of harmony in our ties than ever existed before.

— Memo from Mr. McFarlane to Mr. Reagan on the eve of the summit

Prodded by Canada's Mulroney, Reagan yields on acid rain

From the day he took office, Ronald Reagan refused to acknowledge that man-made pollutants cause acid rain. In 1980, he went so far as to say that acid rain was caused by trees. In a St. Patrick's Day meeting a year ago in Quebec City with Canadian Prime Minister Brian Mulroney, the President rejected requests from his fellow Irishman for U.S. action. But last week in Washington, during his second "shamrock summit" with Mulroney, Reagan changed his tune. "Acid rain," said he, "is a serious concern affecting both our countries."...

— John S. Demott, "The Etchings of Friendship," *Time,* 31 March 1986

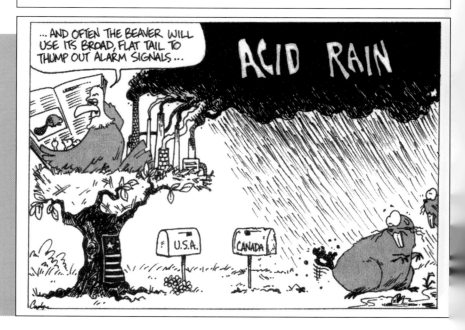

FREE TRADE

"With one signature of a pen... [Brian Mulroney has] thrown us into the north-south influence of the United States."

— John Turner, 1988

"Once a country opens itself up to a subsidy war with the United States in terms of definitions, then the political ability of this country to [resist] the influence of the United States, to remain an independent nation — that has gone forever, and that is the issue of this election… For 120 years, we have done it [created a country with an east-west axis]. With one signature of a pen, you've reversed that, thrown us into the north-south influence of the United States, and will reduce us, will reduce us I am sure, to a colony of the United States, because when the economic levers go, the political independence is sure to follow."

— Liberal Opposition Leader John Turner to PM Brian Mulroney during the 1988 Leaders' debate

"…I maintained that the opponents of the FTA "don't think Canadians can hack it. They don't think Canadians can compete. They're subsidy seekers. They're security-blanket supplicants." I pointed out to Ontario residents that if Newfoundland could survive political and economic integration with mainland Canada without losing its distinctive culture then Ontario and Canada could survive economic integration with the United States without losing our culture if, in fact, Ontario had any culture to lose…."

— John Crosbie, Minister of Trade during the Free Trade Debate

GARNEAU FIRST CANADIAN IN SPACE
October 5, 1984 Cape Canaveral Florida

Marc Garneau…becomes first Canadian in space on board Space Shuttle Challenger Flight STS-41G; during the eight day mission he will travel a total of 3.4 million miles around the Earth in 133 orbits; the crew will deploy the Earth Radiation Budget Satellite, conduct scientific observations of the earth with the OSTA-3 pallet and Large Format Camera (LFC), and demonstrate potential satellite refueling with an EVA and associated hydrazine transfer. Mission duration is 197 hours 23 minutes.

— *Canadian Milestones, 1984.*

▲ Marc Garneau inside the cockpit of the Canadarm Shuttle Simulator at the Johnson Space Center. Garneau had the distinction of being Canada's first astronaut to explore space as part of the American Space Shuttle program.

SOCIAL AND CULTURAL ISSUES

"The Americans had been taught that they were at the centre of the universe, a huge healthy apple pie, with other countries and cultures sprinkled around like raisins. We, on the other hand, had been taught that we were one of the raisins, in fact, the raisin…"

— Margaret Atwood, 1982

"I am not greatly worried by what is called the Americanization of Canada. What people mean when they speak of Americanization has been just as lethal to American culture as it has been to Canadian culture. It's a kind of leveling down which I think every concerned citizen of democracy should fight, whether he is a Canadian or an American."

— Northrop Frye, cultural and literary critic, CBC interview with Robert Fulford, 1984

Serious Violent Crime Rate in Canada and the U.S.
1962-1985 (per 100 000 population)

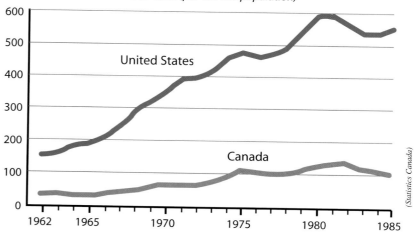

(Statistics Canada)

1990-1999

1990
Canada joins Organization of American States

1990
13 Feb: U.S. and European allies forge agreement with Soviet Union and East Germany on two-stage formula to reunite Germany

INTERNATIONAL EVENTS outside of North America at the beginning of the 1990s had the greatest impact on the relationship between Canada and the United States. In August of 1990, Iraq's Saddam Hussein invaded his oil rich neighbour, Kuwait. The U.S. demanded that Saddam remove his troops from Kuwait. When this demand was ignored, the United Nations, under the leadership of the United States, requested armed action to remove Saddam from Kuwait. After some deliberation, PM Mulroney contributed Canadian personnel and equipment to the conflict. This cemented relations between Mulroney and the new American President, George Bush, for the duration of their political careers.

In back-to-back seasons in 1992 and 1993, the Toronto Blue Jays made history by being the first non-American team to win the World Series. During the first series in 1992, relations between the two countries were briefly soured when U.S. Marines caused the "flag flap" by flying a Canadian flag upside down at a game in Atlanta.

In October 1993, a newly elected Prime Minister, Jean Chrétien, was immediately confronted with the issue of North American economic integration with recently ratified North American Free Trade Agreement (NAFTA). Many of the concerns that were expressed about the impact that the Canada-US Free Trade Agreement had already had on Canadian sovereignty were once again expressed about NAFTA. Feelings were not calmed when the RCMP sold the rights to the traditional Mountie image to Disney in 1995.

The old issue of economic relations with Cuba again created tension between the two neighbours in the middle of the decade. The American Congress passed the Helms-Burton Bill which held Canadian businessmen liable for payments to Americans who lost property in the 1959 Cuban Revolution. Canada protested that this was an illegal application of American law outside of the jurisdiction of the U.S. Two Canadian MPs presented an almost identical bill in Parliament called the Godfrey-Milliken Bill to make American businessmen liable to the descendants of United Empire Loyalists who lost property as a result of the American Revolution. Divergent policies toward Cuba remain a source of diplomatic irritation to this day.

Differences in foreign policy did not stop with Cuba. Canada's Foreign Affairs Minister, Lloyd Axworthy, took a leadership role in two international initiatives — the agreement to ban the sale and use of land mines, and the establishment of a permanent International Criminal Court. By 1997, more that 122 countries had signed the land mine treaty. In August 1998, 120 countries meeting in Rome voted to establish the ICC. However, the United States continues to refuse to ratify either international agreement.

THE NORTH AMERICAN FREE TRADE AGREEMENT (NAFTA)

PREAMBLE

The Government of Canada, the Government of the United Mexican States and the Government of the United States of America, resolved to:...

*CREATE an expanded and secure market for the goods and services produced in their territories;
*REDUCE distortions to trade;
*ESTABLISH clear and mutually advantageous rules governing their trade;
*ENSURE a predictable commercial framework for business planning and investment;...
*CREATE new employment opportunities and improve working conditions and living standards in their respective territories;
*UNDERTAKE each of the preceding in a manner consistent with environmental protection and conservation;...

"I want a foreign policy that will ensure Canada's independence and strength in a multilateral as opposed to a continental framework. I want a foreign policy that secures greater independence in our dealings with the United States...."

— Liberal Party Leadership Candidate Jean Chrétien, "A Modern Foreign Policy," speech to the Empire Club of Canada, 8 Mar 1990

(AP PHOTO/Pat Sullivan)

◄ From left, Mexican President Carlos Salinas de Gortari, U.S. President George Bush, and Canadian PM Brian Mulroney smile as their respective trade representatives initial the North American Free Trade Agreement in San Antonio, Texas, 7 October 1992.

New report shows NAFTA has harmed workers in all three countries

— Economic Policy Institute, Washington, 2001

Assessing Free Trade
Percentage of Canadians saying...

	1990	1999
Canada has benefitted more	4	9
Same effect in both countries	24	17
U.S. has benefitted more	66	63

PROBLEMS WITH THE THIRD OPTION

...1. There was very little will, in government, officialdom or business, to implement the diversification in our foreign relations prescribed by the third option. While the government was exhorting in favour of diversification, economic and trade relations with the U.S. were continuing to deepen. When the third option was proclaimed in 1973, our trade with the U.S. stood at around 60 per cent of our total exports; by 1984, when the Liberal government was defeated, it had reached over 75 per cent.... 2....If anti-Americanism was not a typical state of mind among our diplomats, it is nevertheless the case that, in the decades of the 1970s and 1980s, a number of officers sometimes gave the impression that they judged the legitimacy of our foreign policy by the extent to which it differed from that of the U.S....

— Allan Gotlieb, "The United States in Canadian Foreign Policy" Toronto, 10 December 1991, O.D. Skelton Lecture Series

HELMS-BURTON LAW

(Thomas Boldt 1996)

CANADA AMENDS ORDER BLOCKING U.S. TRADE RESTRICTIONS

…"We have made it clear time and again to the U.S. Congress and Administration that Canada will not tolerate any interference in the sovereignty of Canadian laws.… Canada will continue to monitor actions by the United States to ensure that the interests of Canadian businesses are protected."…

— André Ouellet, Department of Justice Canada, 18 January 1996

A large majority of Canadians (79%), and a plurality of Americans (48%) oppose the Helms-Burton Act

— Angus Reid, Public Release, 8 April 1997

SEC. 102. ENFORCEMENT OF THE ECONOMIC EMBARGO OF CUBA.

(a) Policy.–

(1) Restrictions by other countries.–The Congress hereby reaffirms section 1704(a) of the Cuban Democracy Act of 1992, which states that the President should encourage foreign countries to restrict trade and credit relations with Cuba in a manner consistent with the purposes of that Act.

(2) Sanctions on other countries.–The Congress further urges the President to take immediate steps to apply the sanctions described in section 1704(b)(1) of that Act against countries assisting Cuba.…

U.S. vs. Cuba: Helms-Burton Act Arouses Worldwide Anger

The Clinton administration started implementing the reactionary Helms-Burton Act July 10 by informing high-level executives and shareholders of Sherritt International, a Canadian nickel mining company, that they and their families would be barred from the United States for doing business with Cuba.

Ottawa immediately protested the new law.… In addition, Canadian non-governmental organizations and churches announced their intention to boycott tourism in Florida.… The Helms-Burton Act's real teeth are in the provision that allows U.S. citizens to sue foreign companies and individuals in U.S. courts for profiting from property confiscated by the Cuban government.…

— Teresa Gutierrez, Workers World, 25 July 1996

A Canadian response to the Helms-Burton Law

…The Godfrey-Milliken Bill would permit descendants of the United Empire Loyalists who fled the United States in the years following the 1776 American Revolution to reclaim land that is rightfully theirs and was confiscated unjustly and illegally by the American government and its citizens.…

— Sam Boskey, Infobahn Online Services, 29 October 1996

VIEWS AND VALUES

Shared values, conflicting values	% who agree: Canada	U.S.
The preservation of traditional family values is very important	93	96
All guns should be registered	80	78
No one has the right to impose their morality on others	80	78
It is acceptable for gays to teach school	68	56
We are allowing too many immigrants in	49	58
There is a hell	49	73
Marijuana use should be legalized	45	29
I would not walk alone at night in my community	32	33

Canadians on Americans:	
Overall negative	36
Overall positive	24
Neutral	13

Americans on Canadians:	
Overall positive	40
Overall negative	3
Neutral	19

(Maclean's, 20 December 1999)

"Canada has been a wonderful partner for the United States, and an incredibly important and constructive citizen throughout the entire world…"

— U.S. President Bill Clinton, 25 October 1995

◄ Chrétien and Clinton play golf in Halifax, June 1999. At the end of the game, both leaders would only disclose that the score was a "state secret."

"Canada is the largest country in the world that doesn't exist."

— Richard Rodriguez, American social commentator of Mexican-Indian descent, commenting on the notion that minority groups overtake majority groups, in an interview by Neil Bissoondath on TVO's *Markings,* 3 July 1995

1990 – 1999

ENVIRONMENTAL CONCERNS

"I want a foreign policy that will pursue solutions to the emerging environmental crisis.... [W]e need a system of rules to preserve and protect the world environment. Because of its location in the world, Canada is on the frontline. In the north, we are directly responsible for the Arctic.... In the south, our proximity to the greatest industrial power on earth makes us highly vulnerable to all kinds of pollution. I want Canada in the 1990s to be at the forefront of international initiatives to achieve an international law of the atmosphere. Only if countries work together following the same rules can humanity deal effectively with environmental threats that know no boundaries."

— Liberal Party Leadership Candidate Jean Chrétien, "A Modern Foreign Policy," speech to The Empire Club of Canada, 8 Mar 1990

Report shows significant progress made to clean-up the Great Lakes

..."The Canada-Ontario Agreement (COA) sets aggressive targets for the clean-up of the Great Lakes, the world's largest freshwater system. With the co-operation of all our partners, we have met many of these and made real progress on others," federal Environment Minister David Anderson said. "In the Great Lakes, discharges of contaminants and persistent toxic substances have dropped, as have the levels of persistent toxic substances in fish and wildlife."

— Ministry of the Environment, Government of Ontario News Release, 21 September 1999

THE SALMON WARS

Catch of Whole Pacific Salmon
(thousands of tonnes)

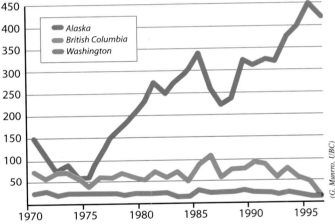

Legend:
- Alaska
- British Columbia
- Washington

(G. Munrro, UBC)

COHO

War broke out on the Pacific Northwest Coast last summer as talks on the Pacific Salmon Treaty collapsed....

Verbal shots have been exchanged across the bow by American and Canadian fishermen near the Alaskan border in 1997 and again this year, including threats by fishermen to occupy the Nanoose underwater missile-testing facility, detain Alaskan cruise ships and block the Alaskan highway.

So why can't two civilized countries with the world's longest undefended border quietly and efficiently manage salmon stocks?

It's a complex concoction of factors: declining prices for salmon, stagnate consumer demand, cuts to Canada's Unemployment insurance program, poor catches due to El Nino that has Canadian fishermen bubbling with desperation.

Alaskan "theft" of Canadian fish is something tangible fishermen can attack, hoping for continued public sympathy and praying for yet another temporary stay of execution by the government...

...The provincial government claims B.C. interception of U.S. salmon has declined 25 per cent since the first salmon treaty in 1985, while the American interception of B.C. salmon has increased by more than 50 per cent during the same period, resulting in a $60-million loss to the provincial economy.... Alaska also argues that Canada's problems are due largely to environmental degradation resulting from poor forestry practices...

— Erik Poole, "The Salmon Wars," *Vancouver Sun*, 25 July 1998

DON'T LET THE GOVERNMENT BREAK ITS PROMISES AND LET US GO EXTINCT!

OMRC (503) 283-6343 x224

KEEP WILD SALMON IN THE PICTURE!

▲ When the 1985 bilateral treaty on fishing restrictions expired, conflicts between Canada and the U.S. over salmon fishery continued.

Pacific salmon deal begins 'era of conservation'

Stocks to be fished depending on abundance — not quotas — under long-awaited pact

The U.S. and Canada declared peace in the Pacific salmon war yesterday, but several B.C. fishing groups are still sniping from the sidelines....

— Charlie Anderson, *The Ottawa Citizen*, 4 June 1999

1997
3 Dec: Up to 120 countries sign ban on land mines in Ottawa — U.S., China, Russia, and Iraq refuse

1998
8-9 Jan: Northeast U.S. and Canada hit with severe ice storm — damage estimated at $350 million

1998
3 June: U.S. and Canada sign 10-year accord to limit salmon fishing in northwest

CONTINENTAL DRIFT

THE RCMP-DISNEY CONTRACT

RCMP-Disney deal not so goofy after all: Thousands have been raised for community policing programs

The RCMP has found that it pays to be a Mickey Mouse operation [t]hree years after the Mounties linked up with Walt Disney Co. to market products bearing their image...

— *Windsor Star*, 29 June 1998

Mickey the Mountie
— *The Ottawa Citizen*, 30 December 1997

MOUNTIES DROP DISNEY: Foundation formed to control licensing force's trademarks

Dudley Do-Right and Snow White are parting ways. The Mounties are taking back control of their image from Walt Disney Co. after a five-year romance....

— Dennis Bueckert, *Montreal Gazette*, 25 September 1999

Should we expect the Disneyfying of everything?

OH, BOTHER... NO BOOK ROYALTIES. NO DISNEY CONTRACT. ...I DIDN'T EVEN GET A VISIT TO THE GARBAGE DUMP!

THE ORIGINAL WINNIPEG THE POOH

(Aislin)

U.S. Trade with Canada
Exports and Imports, Goods, Services and Income, 1988-2000
(billions of U.S. dollars)

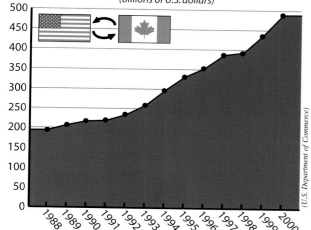

(U.S. Department of Commerce)

THE FOREIGN PUBLISHERS ADVERTISING SERVICES ACT (FPASA) Received Royal Assent on 17 June 1999

The prohibition on foreign publishers selling advertising services aimed primarily at the Canadian market was amended to allow... an exemption that allows foreign publishers to invest in Canada, create new businesses and produce a majority of Canadian content if they want to have greater access to advertising revenues....

% of editorial content that is Canadian	Ads that can be sold by the publisher that are aimed at the Canadian market	Tax deduction to the advertiser of the Ads
less than 50	up to 18	50% of deduction
between 50 & 79	up to 100	50% of deduction
more than 80	up to 100	100% of deduction

(Department of Canadian Heritage)

Swallowing Canadian Companies
Value of U.S. acquisitions of Canadian companies (in billions)

1999 (to Nov. 30)	$25.6
1998	$16.1
1997	$8
1996	$14
1995	$8.8
1994	$5.6

Responses in both countries on the likelihood of Canada and the United States becoming one nation in the next 25 years.

	Likely	Not likely
Canada	32%	66%
U.S.	19%	77%

Half of Canadians say we are becoming more American; one in four wants a U.S. passport.

— "The Vanishing Border," *Maclean's*, 20 December 1999

CONTINENTAL DRIFT...

Harold!...

(Denny Pritchard, 1999/Reprinted with permission –Torstar Syndicate Services)

Into the 21st Century

Day of terror

The number of dead and injured climbs into the thousands and a country is plunged into mourning after hijacked planes are crashed into the World Trade Center in New York and the Pentagon in Washington.

Terrorists turned four commercial airliners into passenger-laden missiles Tuesday, unleashing the deadliest sneak attack against the United States since the bombing of Pearl Harbor…

— *The Guardian* (Charlottetown), 12 September 2001

Out of horror shine decency and goodness

…In praise of heroes Vancouver firefighters initiated a fundraising campaign for the families of their dead "brothers" in New York. The people of Vancouver responded, donating $600 000 within 12 hours.

— *Canada World View*, Department of Foreign Affairs, Winter 2002

Ready to party hearty in Gander

…'We are expecting maybe five or six thousand people…. But if the whole town shows up, I'm ready to feed them.'…

Most astonishing about the event, which will feature local musicians, is that the organizers have no connection to the people in the 38 U.S.-bound planes that landed in Canada on Sept. 11, 2001, after the airspace over the United States was closed.

The Steeleys are throwing the party out of an unabashed generosity based on a desire to thank a community. They raised nearly $54,000 for the cause but expect to pay thousands of dollars worth of bills with their own money….

— Shawna Richer, *The Globe and Mail*, 20 September 2003

U.S. officials bristle at Chrétien 'waffling'

WASHINGTON — Prime Minister Jean Chrétien's tour of the World Trade Center wreckage today should have taken place five days ago as part of his visit to the White House…

— Mike Blanchfield, *Times Colonist* (Victoria), 29 September 2001

(CP PHOTO/Tom Hanson)

▲ Canadian Prime Minister Jean Chrétien, along with *(L to R)* Canadian Alliance leader Stockwell Day, NDP leader Alexa McDonough, and Bloc leader Gilles Duceppe, take in what is left of the World Trade Center at Ground Zero in New York City, 29 September 2001.

BORDER CONTROLS

(Tim Dolighan, 1 April 2003)

"… I'VE HEARD IT'S A BIT CHILLY IF YOU'RE CANADIAN…"

CANADA–U.S. FRIENDSHIP BRIDGE

CANADIANS EXPECT DELAYS!

DOLIGHAN
www.dolighan.com

*Building a **Smart Border** for the 21st century on the foundation of a North American zone of confidence*

The terrorist actions of September 11 were an attack on our common commitment to democracy, the rule of law and a free and open economy. They highlighted a threat to our public and economic security. They require our governments to develop new approaches to meet these challenges. This declaration commits our governments to work together to address these threats to our people, our institutions and our prosperity.

Public security and economic security are mutually reinforcing. By working together to develop a zone of confidence against terrorist activity, we create a unique opportunity to build a smart border for the 21st century; a border that securely facilitates the free flow of people and commerce; a border that reflects the largest trading relationship in the world.

Our countries have a long history of cooperative border management. This tradition facilitated both countries' immediate responses to the attacks of September 11. It is the foundation on which we continue to base our cooperation, recognizing that our current and future prosperity and security depend on a border that operates efficiently and effectively under all circumstances….

— Smart Border Declaration, Canadian Embassy, Washington, 1 July 2003

FACE IT
JOHNNY...
YOU NEED
PROTECTION...

STA[R] WARS II

(Bruce MacKinnon, Halifax Herald, 2000)

Missile plan splits Canada, U.S.

Shock in Washington: Putin nominates Ottawa as mediator in shield standoff

— *National Post*, 19 Dec 2000

ON GUARD FOR THE FUTURE:

The threat of terrorism remains and Canada must share in the defence

One year after North America awoke to the horror of terrorism, this continent is just beginning to understand the full scope of the threat....

— *Calgary Herald*, 11 September 2002

"[A] fundamental consideration for Canada must be our interest in the future of NORAD…which since 1958 has served us well for the joint defence of this continent.... If missile defence is an exclusively American project and thus remains outside of NORAD, the role and relevance of this partnership, so crucial to our participation in the defence of North America, will come into question....[I]f we do not discuss these issues…we will be surrendering our voice, in fact our sovereignty, and ceding to the United States the role of unilaterally determining the shape of the defence of North America...."

— Foreign Affairs Minister Bill Graham, address, House of Commons debate on Ballistic Defence, Ottawa, 15 May 2003

No American rockets should be stationed on Canadian turf. We can tolerate tracking stations. We built the Distant Early Warning (DEW) line in the 1950s to detect missiles and aircraft. But we stopped stationing U.S. interceptor weapons on our soil decades ago. Let's keep it that way.

— Editorial, *Toronto Star*, 17 May 2003

What should the U.S. do to influence Canadian defense policy?

While the U.S. never feared that Canada would not cooperate in countering terrorism in North America the border control case is interesting for what it may tell the U.S. about how to…secure increased Canadian government support for the Canadian Forces....

In the case of the border, the root of success may have been U.S. specificity.... This made it easier for Canada to make decisions. And it probably made it harder to resist the U.S. ideas because they were clearly stated and easily understandable to both the Government and the public. In the case of defense, however, the U.S. has not been specific.... [U]rgings to spend more or some fraction of GDP, lack of insistence on missile defense combined with well-deserved compliments on the effectiveness of particular units of the Canadian Forces are not a clear message....

In the end, however, the future of the U.S.-Canadian defense relationship lies in the hands of the Government of Canada. Their decisions on the future of the Canadian Forces and on missile defense will determine the nature and extent of the U.S.-Canadian military relationship in the future. Events are moving quickly. Canada risks being left behind and left out.

— Dwight N. Mason, draft presentation, Washington, 2003

FRIENDLY FIRE INCIDENT—AFGHANISTAN

Four Canadian soldiers killed, 8 injured in 'friendly fire' accident

OTTAWA (CP) - Four Canadian soldiers were killed and eight injured when an American plane bombed them in Afghanistan in what Canadian authorities termed a tragic accident. Of the injured, two had life threatening wounds, one was in very serious condition while the other five were seriously hurt, said Canadian Forces officials...

— John Ward, 18 April 2002

Friendly fire pilots to escape harsh penalties

Although they once faced the possibility of a 64-year jail sentence, Major William Umbach will simply get a reprimand and his flying partner, Major Harry Schmidt, will face a light set of administrative penalties for the late-night bombing last year that left four Canadian soldiers dead.

The U.S. military announced yesterday that it would not have recourse to a court-martial against the F-16 pilots, saying that any punishment will be meted out through non-judicial means.

— Daniel Leblanc, *Globe and Mail*, 20 June 2003

(AP Photo/Diether Endlicher)

▲ Canadian soldiers, injured in the "friendly fire" training accident in Afghanistan, salute as the remains of their comrades arrive at Ramstein air base, Germany, 20 April 2002.

(U.S. Department of Commerce)

U.S. Trade with Leading Partners	
Exports and Imports, Goods, Services and Income, 2000 (billions of dollars)	
Canada	$489
Japan	322
United Kingdom	301
Mexico	293
Germany	152

(Maclean's, 9 September 2002)

How favourable or unfavourable would you be to Canada abandoning its currency to adopt the American dollar?	
Very favourable	14%
Somewhat favourable	19
Somewhat unfavourable	18
Very unfavourable	45

New Realities at the Canada-U.S. Border

A million dollars of trade takes place between Canada and the United States every minute — $1.7 billion a day — and there are 200 million border crossings a year. To put it in perspective, the U.S. does more two-way trade across the Ambassador Bridge between Windsor and Detroit than it does with any other country. We sell more of our industrial output — 63% — to the U.S. than we consume at home, making Canada our own second-largest market. In total, the Americans buy about 83% of our exports of goods and services... Over 72% of the goods and services we import...come from the U.S. What's more, the U.S. is Canada's primary source of foreign investment. It accounts for 64% of foreign investment here and 58 % of total foreign investment stocks in this country.

— Canadian Manufacturers and Exporters, 26 February 2002

U.S. Imports and Exports
2000 (billions of U.S. dollars)

Legend:
- U.S. Imports of Goods from Canada
- U.S. Exports of Goods to Canada

(Categories: Transportation, Energy Products, Forest Products, Equipment & Tools, Telecommunications, Metals, Chemicals, Machinery, Agriculture, Other)

SOFTWOOD LUMBER

Canada's dispute with the United States over softwood lumber is estimated to have cost lumber producers up to $1.5 billion and thousands of jobs.

And even though the World Trade Organization ruled in May 2003 in support of Canada's position — that Canadian stumpage programs aren't subsidies — Washington has a chance to appeal the decision.

Stumpage fees are set amounts charged to companies that harvest timber on public land. The fees have long been at the heart of the long-running dispute. Many in the U.S. see them as being too low, making them de facto subsidies. A U.S. coalition of lumber producers wants the provincial governments to follow the American system and auction off timber rights at market prices....

The dispute came to a head in August 2001 when the Bush administration backed a U.S. forest industry bid to hit Canadian lumber with billions of dollars in duties. This meant that Canadians exporting south of the border were charged a 19.3 per cent countervailing duty — essentially a tax applied to imports deemed to have been unfairly subsidized. The penalty was increased two months later when the government imposed a further anti-dumping duty of 12.57 per cent....

— Amina Ali, Sabrina Saccoccio and Justin Thompson, "Softwood Lumber Dispute," CBC News Online, Web Posted March 2001

NAFTA panel upholds U.S. lumber tariffs

But U.S. calculation of anti-dumping duties found to be wrong

A North American Free Trade Agreement panel upheld American tariffs on lumber imports from Canada Thursday, but said the U.S. department of commerce was wrong in its calculation of some anti-dumping...

— Greg Mercer, *Vancouver Sun,* 18 July 2003

♪ WE STAND ON GUARD ♫ FOR THEE!

LOUDER.

WTO Reaffirms U.S. Wrong In Giving Fines From Foreign Trade To American Companies

— *The Guardian* (Charlottetown), 17 January 2003

Softwood-Lumber Dispute Hurts U.S. Home Buyers And Canadian Workers: Cost Includes 7,000 Jobs Lost In Quebec And Fewer Americans Able To Afford Homes

— *Montreal Gazette,* 25 January 2003

SAME-SEX MARRIAGES

Gay marriages in Canada expected to become another U.S. pressure point

Gay activists in the U.S. are serving notice that Canada's plan to legalize same-sex marriage will put pressure on their state and federal governments to follow suit...

— Janice Tibbetts, *Vancouver Sun,* 20 June 2003

Canada's 'I do' to gay marriage gives U.S. couples new hope

— *The Halifax Daily News,* 22 June 2003

…What is obscured by this frenzy of condemnation of anti-Americanism is that there is a very vocal minority in this country who are so pro-American, so enamoured by the current U.S. administration, that they have essentially become anti-Canadians…. The anti-Canadians simply don't like Canada because it is so unlike the U.S. in so many ways…

Any Canadian policy that deviates even slightly from the American model comes under attack. Universal health care? Privatize it. Gun control? Trash it? Kyoto? We can't implement it if the U.S. hasn't.

When it comes to the war on terrorism, Canadians may be on the front lines in Afghanistan, but the anti-Canadians are ashamed and mortified by Canada's unwillingness to join George Bush's invasion of Iraq….

— Dimitry Anastakis, a fulbright visiting scholar at Michigan State University, *Toronto Star,* 27 March 2003

◄ Anti-war protesters in Calgary. Tens of thousands joined anti-war demonstrations across Canada. Others joined demonstrations in support of the American-led War on Iraq.

Canada's Chrétien defends staying out of war

…"Close friends can disagree at times and still remain close friends," Chrétien told parliament… The U.S. government has expressed disappointment over Canada's failure to support the war, and Canadian business leaders have warned of unfavorable trade policies, canceled business deals and reduced tourism as retaliation.

Chrétien said he sought to give U.N. weapons inspectors more time to try to disarm Iraq.

"The decision on whether or not to send troops into battle must always be a decision of principle, not a decision of economics, not even a decision of friendship alone… While we are not participating in the coalition…let us be very clear this government and all Canadians hope for a quick victory for the U.S.-led coalition with the minimum of casualties."…

— Tom Cohen, 8 April 2003

Hundreds of anti-war protesters chanting "Drop Bush, not bombs" and "No blood for oil" marched through downtown St. John's in tandem with thousands of like-minded peace activists around the world…

— Brian Callahan, *The Telegram* (St. John's), 23 March 2003

Bush cancels visit to Canada
Ottawa 'muddling along': Decision not to hand over Iraqis called final straw

George W. Bush has cancelled a planned visit to Canada on May 5 because of unhappiness over Ottawa's stance on the war in Iraq and anti-American comments by members of the Chrétien government, sources say….

One source said the final straw for the White House was the Prime Minister's order to the Canadian commander in charge of a multilateral naval task force in the Persian Gulf that fugitive members of the Iraqi regime must not be turned over to U.S. forces….

— Robert Fife, Ottawa Bureau Chief, *National Post,* 12 April 2003

America Lite: Is That Our Future?

Not like them. It's how we've defined ourselves for generations. Quieter, less violent, more caring, not as arrogant. Different. Better. Everything Americans are, we aren't….

We whine when America ignores us. We bellow with rage when they pay too much attention….

…Today, 58 per cent of Canadians still believe our quality of life is superior to that of our American neighbours, but take a long look around. Gunplay in the streets of our major cities is no longer a rarity. Homelessness is a national crisis. Food banks are a permanent fixture in communities across the country. Free trade has made the border (at least for goods) practically a thing of the past. Eatons and Front *Page Challenge* have been replaced by the Gap and *American Idol.* Our foreign policies are almost indistinguishable. Culturally, commercially, politically, Canada and the United States are closer than ever….

– by Jonathon Gatehouse, *Maclean's,* 25 November 2002

Strong and Free

…Most of us can remember the exact moment when we realized the Americans don't like us anymore. It was during the post-9/11 Bush address to Congress when he stopped to thank America's very best friend in the entire universe…England. Huh? And then their next best friend, Mexico, and then somewhere between Cameroon and Cape Verde came to Canada….

– Douglas Coupland, *Maclean's,* 25 November 2002

CN's branding strategy draws fire from Ottawa
Having made inroads into U.S. markets, railway wants to shed the word 'Canadian'

Only weeks after the Toronto Blue Jays caught flak for ditching the Maple Leaf, another national icon, Canadian National Railway, is drawing fire for dropping the word "Canadian" from everyday corporate use…. This is a great Canadian institution, one of the best railways in North America, and we should not apologize for being Canadian, the Transport Minister [David Collenette] said….

— Steven Chase, *Globe and Mail,* 20 September 2003

(Courtesy of CN)

Glossary

A

Acid Rain 37, 38
Afghanistan 45, 47
Alaska Boundary 8, 9
Alaska-Canadian Highway 20, 21
All-Star Game 41
Alouette I 29
American Civil War 4, 6
American Investment 35
American League 41
American Revolution 4, 6
Amundsen, Roald 10
Anderson, David 42
Anti-Cruise Missile 37
Arctic Sovereignty 31
Arctic Waters Pollution Act 31
Atlee, Clement 22
Atomic Bomb 20, 22
Atwood, Margaret 39
Auto Pact 28, 30
Avro Arrow 24, 26, 27
AWACS 31
Axis Powers 20
Axworthy, Lloyd 40

B

Baby Boom 20
Banting and Best 15
Battle of Little Big Horn 7
Bennett, R.B. 18, 19
Bentley, Elizabeth 22
Bentsen, Edgar 35
Berton, Pierre 32
Bilingualism 28
Bomarc 24, 27, 28, 29
Border Controls 44
Boston Marathon 8
Boundary Waters Treaty 34
Branch Plants 15, 25, 28, 35
British North America 4, 6
British North American Act 4
Broadcasting Act 31
Blum, Barbara 34
Burns, Tommy 10
Bush, George 40, 47

C

Canadarm 36, 39
Canada Council 24, 26
Canadian Astronaut Program 36
Canadian Air Force 37
Carter, Jimmy 32
Castro, Fidel 32
CBC 5, 32
CBS 24
CCF 18, 25
Chief Sitting Bull 7
Chrétien, Jean 40, 41, 42, 44, 47
Churchill, Winston 19, 21
Civil Rights 24
Clark, Joe 32
Clinton, Bill 41
Cold War 20, 23, 24, 37
Columbia River Treaty 29
Confederation 6, 32, 36
Connor, Ralph 17
Continental Drift 34
Crosbie, John 39
CRTC 5, 31, 32
Cruise Missile Crisis 37
Cuban Missile Crisis 28, 29
Cuban Revolution 40

D

Day, Stockwell 44
D-Day 20, 21, 23
Democrats 18
Depression 18, 20
Devil's Brigade 20

DEW (Distant Early Warning) Line 24, 27
Diefenbaker PM 26, 27, 28, 29
Dionne Quintuplets 18
Dofasco 25
Douglas, Tommy 30
Draft Dodgers 32
Duceppe, Gilles 44

E

Eisenhower, Dwight 27
EXPO '67 30

F

Fascism 18, 23
FBI 20, 22, 33
Flood, Daniel J. 29
Ford, Gerald 32, 35
Foreign Investment Review Act 34, 35
Foreign Investment Review Agency 32, 35, 38
Fowler Commission 25
FPASA (Foreign Publishers Advertising Services Act) 43
FTA (Free Trade Agreement) 5, 36, 39

G

Garneau, Marc 36, 38, 39
Gast, John 6
General Motors 19
Geneva Summit 37
Godfrey-Milliken Bill 40, 42
Gordon Royal Commission 26
Gordon, Walter 25
Gouzenko, Igor 22, 23
Graham, Bill 45
Great Lakes Water Quality Agreement 34
Québecois 28

H

Halibut Treaty 14
Helms-Burton Bill 40, 41, 42
Hiroshima 20, 22
Hockey Hall of Fame 29
Howe, C.D. 24, 25
Hull, Cordell 18
Humphrey, John 20
Hussein, Saddam 40
Hutchinson, Bruce 31
Hyde Park Declaration 20, 21

I

I'm Alone 15
International Boundary Waters Treaty 7, 8
International Boundary Waters Treaty Act 10
International Criminal Court 40
International Joint Commission 34
International Waterways Commission 10
Investment Canada 38
Iraq 47

J

Japanese Canadians 21
Jeffrey, Brian 27
Joint Board of Defence 20
Joint Defence 45
Johnson, Lyndon 30
Juno Beach 21, 23

K

Kennedy, John F. 28, 29
King, Mackenzie 15, 18, 19, 22, 23
Kitty Hawk 9
Korean War 24

L

Labour Unions 19
Land Mines 40
Laurier, Wilfrid 7, 8, 10, 11

League of Nations 14
Lend-Lease 20
Litton Industries 36, 37
Long, Huey 18
Longboat, Tom 10
Loyalists 6

M

Major League Baseball 31
Manhattan Project 20, 22, 23
Manifest Destiny 4, 6
Marconi, Guglielmo 9
Marshall Plan 23
Massey Commission 24
Massey, Vincent 23, 24
McCarthy, Joe 20
McCarthy, Leighton 22
McCurdy, John 11
McDonald's 30
McDonough, Alexa 44
McKenzie, Vernon 15
Minifie, James M. 26
Meighen, Arthur 19
Monroe Doctrine 4, 6
Mulroney, Brian 36, 37, 38, 39, 40
Multiculturism 28

N

NAFTA (North American Free Trade Agreement) 5, 40, 42, 46
Nagasaki 20, 22
NASA 36
National Energy Program 36
National Identity 47
National League 41
National Library 24
National Policy 10
Nationalism 28, 32, 35, 36
NATO (North Atlantic Treaty Organisation) 20, 23
Naval Service Bill 11
Nazism 20, 23
NFB 24
NHL 16
Nobel Peace Prize 25
NORAD (North American Air/Aerospace Defence Command) 24, 26, 29, 36, 37, 45
Northwest Passage 31
Niagara Falls 17
Nixon 33, 34
Nuclear Debate 29

O

Ogdensburg Agreement 20
Olympics 19, 35, 39,
Ouellet, André 41
Oshawa Strike 19
Owen, Jesse 19

P

Peace Bridge 17
Pearl Harbor 20, 21
Pearson, L 22, 25, 27, 28, 29, 30
Pipeline Debate 24, 25
Polio Vaccine 24 30
Prohibition 13, 14, 16
Protectionism 18
Putin, V. 45

Q

Quebec Conference 21
Queen Elizabeth II 27
Quiet Diplomacy 30

R

Radisson/Tomahawk 24
Randall, Stanley 25
RCMP 40, 43

Reagan, Ronald 36, 37, 38
Reciprocity Treaty 7, 8, 10, 11, 12
Republicans 18
Riel, Louis 4
Ritchie, Charles 22
Roosevelt, Franklin 15, 18, 19, 20
Rose, Fred 20
Royal Commission on Economic Prospects 25
Royal Commission on National Development in the Arts, Letters, and Sciences 24
Royal Commission on Publications 28

S

Salmon Wars 42
Same-Sex Marriages 46
San Francisco Conference 22
Shamrock Summit 37, 38
Sheardowns, John 36
Slavery 4, 7
Slotkin, Louis 23
Social Credit Party 18
Sovereignty Association 36
Smoot-Hawley Tariff Act 18
Softwood Lumber 46
Space Shuttle Challenger 36, 38
Space Shuttle Columbia 36
St. Laurent, Louis 23
St. Lawrence Seaway 19, 24, 26, 27
Stalin 23
Stock Market Crash 14, 17, 18
Strategic Defense Initiative 37
Suez Crisis 25
Suffield Coalition Rally 33

T

Taft, W.H. 11
Tariff 10
Taylor, Ken 32, 36
Terrorists 44, 45, 47
The Guess Who 32
Tonkin Gulf 29
Toronto Blue Jays 40, 42
Trans-Canada Pipelines 25
Treaty of Ghent 6
Treaty of Paris 6
Treaty of Versailles 13, 14
Trudeau, Pierre 28, 30, 31, 33, 34, 35, 36
Truman, Harry 22, 23
Turner, John 39

U

Union Nationale 18
United Automobile Workers 19, 38
United Nations 22, 47
Universal Declaration of Human Rights 20
U.S. Congress 8

V

Versailles Conference 8
Vietnam War 30, 32, 33

W

War Measures Act 33
Watkins Report 30
Weapons Inspectors 47
World Exposition 38
World Security Charter 22
World Series 40, 42
World Trade Center 44
Wilson, Woodrow 8, 12, 13
Wright, Wilbur and Orville 9

Z

Zurakowski, Jan 26